"DONE GONE EXPANDED"

George Washington Dewey—I cannot tell a lie, Granther. I took them with my little cruiser. We've already got them. The question is, what are we going to do with them. Don't think you mentioned that.

This cartoon by "Bart" (Charles L. Bartholomew) originally appeared in the Minneapolis *Journal* on January 10, 1899.

Primary Sources In American History

CONSULTING EDITOR
Grady McWhiney, University of British Columbia

SLAVERY IN AMERICA:
Theodore Weld's American Slavery As It Is
  Richard O. Curry and **Joanna Dunlap Cowden**

AMERICAN UTOPIANISM
  Robert S. Fogarty

IMPERIALISTS vs ANTI-IMPERIALISTS

THE DEBATE OVER EXPANSIONISM IN THE 1890'S

RICHARD E. WELCH, JR.

LAFAYETTE COLLEGE, EASTON, PA.

F. E. PEACOCK PUBLISHERS, INC.

ITASCA, ILLINOIS

JOHN W. CAUGHEY, Advisory Editor

Foreword

It is not easy to understand the past. A good textbook helps by providing what its author — usually a distinguished historian — considers the essential facts and his interpretation of those facts. A good instructor also helps. But the student, if he is to be other than a parrot, must be exposed to more than one or two viewpoints. Told that authorities disagree, the student is likely to ask: "But which interpretation is *right*?"

At that point he is ready to do some research himself — to read and to evaluate what certain persons who actually saw an event wrote about it. Sampling original sources on which historical interpretations are based is not only an exciting experience; it adds flavor to knowledge. Furthermore, it encourages the student to weigh conflicting evidence himself and to understand historical variety and complexity.

The Primary Sources in American History series provides the documents necessary to explore the past through the eyes of those who lived it. Edited and introduced by an able scholar, each volume in the series contains contemporary material on some historical topic or period — either a collection of varied sources (letters, diaries, memoirs, reports, etc.), or a new edition of a classic eyewitness account.

Grady McWhiney
Editor

Table of Contents

The Philippines and the Debate at Flood Tide

The Panama Canal and the Debate Continued

Territorial Expansion and Commercial Gain

Imperialism and the Needs of Military Defense

ix

Introduction

For its contemporaries it was the Great Debate, and though certain historians today would diminish its substance and importance, it is by no means certain that they should succeed. Americans in the 1890's probably exaggerated the dimensions of the contest over territorial expansion, but there can be little doubt that they were honestly convinced that they were grappling with an issue of great significance for the American Republic. On both sides there was the belief that America stood at the crossroads, and that a policy of colonial acquisition would mark a new era in the history of the nation.

Those who favored the acquisition of overseas territories and protectorates saw expansion as essential to the continued health of the institutions and economy of the republic. The industrial maturity of the American economy demanded controlled foreign markets for American goods and capital; the responsibilities of American diplomacy and security required the acquisition of coaling stations, naval bases, and other instruments of diplomatic and military leverage. Those who opposed the acquisition of overseas territories and

1

protectorates were convinced that expansion would undermine the institutions and moral health of the nation.
Trade would best expand through the peaceful instrumentalities of commerce; colonies would be an economic burden and a diplomatic danger. America could
not maintain its diplomatic independence from the entanglements of power politics if it wasted its strength in
imitation of the colonial greed of the nations of Europe.

Both sides believed they were correctly inter-
preting the needs and unique mission of America;
both sides saw the decision that faced America in the
late 1890's as a decision of crucial importance; both
sides were convinced that they stood diametrically opposed and that the future well-being of America rested
on their success.

Over the past decade various historians have sought
to reduce the scope and significance of the debate over
expansionism in the 1890's. They see it as composed of
inflated rhetoric and little substance, a debate fought by
fellow Expansionists who differed over tactics and instrumentalities. In their eyes both the Imperialists and
the Anti-Imperialists were motivated by a desire for
foreign markets to absorb an expanding surplus of
American fibers and manufactures, and the contestants
differed only in their opinions respecting the necessity
of accompanying economic imperialism with the for-
malities of colonial rule. If these historians stop short of
categorizing the debate as a piece of shadowboxing
between Tweedledum and Tweedledee, they are prepared to insist that the aims and intentions of both sides
were essentially similar. They see the debate over the
March of the Flag as relatively meaningless; for, in

their eyes, both sides were victims of national pride and ambition, both sides saw in the exploitation of foreign peoples and markets a means of avoiding social tensions and problems at home, both sides assumed the implicit virtue of the extended dominion of American industrial capitalism and American cultural values.

This interpretation is not without a certain validity as respects the views of particular contestants of the Great Debate, but as a general characterization of that debate it is fundamentally false. In the final analysis it seems to implant in the minds of the men of the 1890's the experience and guilt complex of the post-World War II generation. It is possible, and indeed useful, to seek historical perspective to current controversies respecting the responsibilities of American foreign policy by evaluating the diplomacy of past generations; it is less helpful to approach the debate over the acquisition of the Philippine Islands by way of the diplomacy of John Foster Dulles.

There were valid distinctions of policy embodied in the debate between the Imperialists and Anti-Imperialists of the 1890's. That these differences were not as extreme as certain of their respective champions claimed disproves neither the sincerity of the contestants nor their conviction that they were participants in a national policy decision of major significance. Their debate must be understood within the historical context of its time. It can profitably be studied only by shedding present-day obsessions, whether of Pax Americana or Neo-Isolationism, and seeking to gain an understanding of the goals and motives of its participants by evaluating the contemporary record — the articles, diaries, speeches, letters, editorials in which they sought to persuade their friends and enemies and themselves of the crucial necessity or mortal danger of expansion.

The expansion which they debated was not a vague economic imperialism but the expansion of American political sovereignty and territorial rule to noncontiguous, overseas territories such as the Samoan Islands, Hawaii, Puerto Rico, Cuba, and the Philippines. The acquisition of an overseas island empire was the topic of their debate.

Only in the last years of the decade of the 1890's did this topic take precedence in the politics and press of America, but talk of insular expansion did not begin with the Spanish-American War. It was foreshadowed — if vaguely — by the abortive effort of the Pierce Administration in the 1850's to acquire Cuba and the unsuccessful labors of Ulysses S. Grant to annex Santo Domingo, some two decades later. Down to the late 1880's, however, expansionism in American history had been essentially linked to the continent of North America. Efforts in behalf of insular acquisition were not without precedent, but they were outside the accustomed boundaries and intentions of American expansionism. In this sense, they would clearly represent a "New Departure" in the diplomatic history of the United States.

At first it was but a handful of publicists and naval officers who projected visions of American flags whipping in the tropic breezes of the Caribbean and the Pacific. Only as the decade of the nineties moved towards its conclusion did insular expansionism become a movement possessed of perceptible popular support, and even then no single component of the American public — not the manufacturers, the merchant importers, or the investors of capital — was united in urging the acquisition of an overseas colonial empire. Movements, however, need not have the allegiance of a clear majority to begin or to succeed, only to continue and survive. As the nineties wore on, the voices of missionaries in search of converts, politicians in search of allegiance, and investors in search of markets joined the early propagandists of naval power and diplomatic activism to form a pressure bloc of growing size and influence. Their activities served both to prepare the way for the acquisition of a respectably large island empire and to help assure its acceptance by an uncertain but sufficient portion of the American public.

The first gain, a portion of the Samoan Islands under a strange tripartite protectorate arrangement with England and Germany in 1889, came perhaps as much by accident as by design. It was only during the initial struggle over the acquisition of Hawaii in the years 1892–93 that battle lines were first drawn. Thwarted at the time, the Expansionists subsequently enlarged their arguments and their appeal. With the return of the Republicans to power in the election of 1896, they were prepared to resume the battle. It is probable if not certain that the wet-eyed tact and political skills of William McKinley would have secured the annexation of Hawaii even in the absence of the war with Spain. That war, however, provided the Expansionists with their great opportunity. As it fed their appetites for colonial gain, so it made such gain increasingly likely.

To state this obvious fact is not to imply that the war itself was the product of expansionist designs or maneuvers, for it was not. The origins of the Spanish-American War lay primarily in the realms of moral humanitarianism and political partisanship. American citizens, wearied of the lengthy and unsettling Cuban insurrection, were outraged by what they judged to be Spanish brutality in Cuba, and Republican politicians, concerned for the success of their party, were afraid of giving their political opponents a popular issue. There was no "Large Policy," and indeed little diplomatic calculation of any sort, involved in America's decision to go to war in 1898.

With that decision, however, the acceleration of expansionist aims was almost inevitable. Victory encouraged territorial ambition. Securing Hawaii by joint congressional resolution while the war was still in progress, the Expansionists demanded after the Armistice that Puerto Rico and the Philippines be retained as spoils of war. Some of the more ambitious also favored the acquisition of the Carolines and the Marianas in the Pacific and the Danish West Indies and possibly Cuba itself in the Caribbean. The growth of the demands and volume of the Expansionists made inevitable in turn the welding of the Anti-Expansionists into a coherent and increasingly vocal bloc. With its formation, the Great Debate was formally declared.

In this debate both sides were marked by a diversity of membership; America did not automatically line up by class, section, party, or occupational self-interest. It is this diversity that lends doubt to explanations of allegiance that confine their attention to economic motivation. There was a diversity of motives in both ranks and, in partial consequence of this fact, a variety of ingredients in the arguments of both the Imperialists and their opponents.

The imperialist argument embraced questions of constitutionality, national defense, diplomatic safety, international duty, and economic gain, and its supporters varied in the emphasis and attention they gave these various ingredients. Orville H. Platt, senior senator from Connecticut, was content to show that the Constitution imposed no legal limitations on the authority of Congress to acquire island territories and hold them in a state of colonial dependence, and by denying the unconstitutionality of a policy of overseas acquisition proved to his own satisfaction its sufficient wisdom. His colleague, Henry Cabot Lodge of Massachusetts, projected a far broader defense of imperialism. America must demand its rights and play its destined role as a world power. It must assume a greater burden of responsibility for the spread of civilization through the dark corners of the world. The needs of diplomatic authority demanded a nation possessed of increased means of military power and defense. America must have naval bases and coaling stations; she must control essential sea-lanes and a transisthmian canal. Only so could she perform in the 20th century the role necessary to her responsibilities to civilization and to her own well-being. There was no option to growth but decay.

Other Expansionists such as Albert J. Beveridge of Indiana gave still greater emphasis to the economic gains to be secured by insular expansionism. A colonial empire would assure the economic growth of America by providing rich sources of industrial raw materials

and markets for American manufactures. Pacific outposts, moreover, would serve as the vestibule for an
expanded trade with the Orient. Such outposts would
provide the equivalent of the "spheres of influence"
being carved from the Celestial Empire by the powers
of Europe and would assure that America was not
denied its proper share of the presumably limitless Chinese market of tomorrow.

And then there were Expansionists who would emphasize the religious obligation imposed on America to
export the liberating truths of Protestant Christianity. If
rhetoric of this sort served some as but a veil for more
secular motives, for others this aim formed the essential
thrust of their conviction of the righteousness of expansion. Still others spoke of the special mission of the
Anglo-Saxon race, the "traditional" nature of expansion, and the immutable obligations placed on the
most fit by the operations of Social Darwinism in the
international sphere. For most, of course, no single
ingredient sufficed; no single motive inspired their convictions. They sought to convince others as well as
themselves, and as the debate continued propaganda
and belief became inextricably entangled.

The same could be said of their opponents. Most of
the Anti-Imperialists stressed above all else the moral
error and danger of expansionism, but their argument
came eventually to embrace economic and strategic
contentions as well as the ingredients of morality, tradition, and diplomatic safety. If their motives were less
diverse than those of their opponents, their composition
was even more heterogeneous and their chief spokesmen exhibited considerable diversity in their particular
concerns and emphases.

George Frisbie Hoar, senior senator from Massachusetts, emphasized the dangerous impropriety of imperialism for a democratic republic where the legitimacy of political authority rested on the consent of the governed. A republic could only have citizens, never subjects; imperialism abroad must undermine liberty at home. The Harvard philosopher William James agreed that America was in danger of needlessly repudiating its special place among nations — was about "to puke up its heritage" — but James gave equal attention to the probability that American expansion would corrupt the existing social systems and values of the island natives. Edward Atkinson, a Boston industrialist, confined his concern to the dangers facing his fellow citizens and stressed both the economic burdens and physical dangers of tropical rule. Overseas imperialism would double the national debt and increase the citizen's tax burden as the result of escalating military expenditures and a greatly bloated bureaucracy. Our soldiers and administrators would prove ill-adapted to the climate of tropical lands, and their bodies and their morals would suffer equal damage. Sam Gompers also attacked the economic errors of imperialism, but his criticisms were more specific and more materialistic in orientation than those of Atkinson. For Gompers the free import of island products, such as tobacco, and the unrestricted immigration of coolie labor posed a major threat to the economic well-being of the American workingman and so to the health of the American economy.

Other commentators stressed the diplomatic dangers of imperialism. America would be militarily weakened, not strengthened, by attempting to guard and control distant territories. Not only would there be the constant danger of native insurrections, but the islands would serve as a potential hostage were we to have diplomatic difficulties with Japan or some European naval power. By entangling ourselves in the diplomatic struggles of the Eastern Hemisphere we would, moreover, be less able to sustain the Monroe Doctrine in the Western Hemisphere.

No member of the articulate band of Anti-Imperialists failed to quote the Declaration of Independence or failed to compare the politicians of the present unfavorably with the statesmen of the past, but their motives and their emphases were far more varied than is usually recognized.

Particularly did the Anti-Imperialists vary in their degrees of racial prejudice and their attitudes respecting the island natives. For some the Malays and Tagalogs were noble victims of injustice; for others they formed a very part of the threat and danger of insular expansionism. In general there was more of racist attitudes and prejudice in the ranks and arguments of the Expansionists than of their opponents, but such Anti-Imperialists as E. L. Godkin, editor of *The Nation,* were undoubtedly convinced that the "men of tropical climes" were innately inferior and that acquisition of their homelands would risk contagion as well as perpetrate injustice. Even the more tolerant of the Anti-Imperialists tended to mix their conviction of the right of all men to political self-determination with a certain patronizing air of *noblesse oblige,* but once again there were exceptions. William James considered the term "Little Brown Brother" both ridiculous and insulting.

It is the variety of arguments and emphases among

the Imperialists and Anti-Imperialists alike that lends interest to the struggle over insular expansionism. It is the intention of this small collection of source materials to illustrate that variety and, hopefully, to further that interest.

Before describing the specific aims and format of this volume, it might be well to indicate what it is not.

This book is not designed to review previous historical explanations of the expansionist fervor and debate of the 1890's nor to offer a new explanation. There have been many brilliant evaluations made of the expansionism of the 1890's and its origins, and particularly those offered by Julius Pratt, Frederick Merk, Richard Hofstadter, Walter La Feber, and Ernest May. An interesting collection could be made indeed of their contrasting analyses. The focus of the volume at hand, however, is upon the participants of a policy struggle not a historiographical dispute. The debate under review is that waged by the politicians, editors, and publicists of the 1890's, as seen through their eyes, as described in their words. The reader is not asked to take any participant at his word but to hear his convictions and rationalizations in his own voice.

It follows that this volume makes no pretext to evaluate the degree of wisdom and foresight of either side. Emphasis is placed on the significance of the battle for its contemporaries, not for later generations. By the same token this collection makes no effort to illustrate parallels between the policy concerns of today and those of the 1890's. It will be obvious to the reader that certain fears expressed by the Anti-Imperialists of the late 1890's respecting the overextension of American

diplomatic commitments bear at least a linguistic relationship to the apprehensions of present-day critics of
American "globalism." More specifically, one can see
in the foreign policy controversies of the two periods a
parallel concern for the impact of military expansion on
domestic institutions and even a similarity of sorts between "pacification" problems in the Philippines and
those some two generations later in Vietnam. This collection is designed, however, not to emphasize such
historical parallels but rather to review within the context of its own time one of the more intelligently and
passionately argued debates in the history of the American people.

It is this aim which has dictated the volume's format
and structure.

Without any pretense of originality, this collection of
contemporary documents has been organized to move
from the general to the particular. The first section
offers two contrasting essays which analyze the nature
of territorial expansion and its relation to the historical
mission of the American Republic. The conclusions
reached are diametrically opposite, but the *Forum* articles of Civil Service Commissioner John R. Procter
and Professor William Graham Sumner both seek to
place the question of overseas expansion against the
background of the American past and within the frame-
work of contemporary world politics.

There follow four case studies of the expansionist
debate as it evolved and accelerated over the years of
the 1890's and into the 20th century. The first of these
studies concerns American participation in a tripartite
protectorate over the Samoan Islands in 1889. Al-

though it occasioned no great stir in the American press, the comments of certain editorial writers foreshadowed the debate to come and expressed in part the subsequent arguments of the friends and foes of expansion. The editors of the New York *Tribune* and the Springfield *Republican* were among the more perceptive in noting the precedent-setting quality of American intervention in the Samoan Islands, as indicated by the editorials selected from each paper.

Hawaii provided a second and more important stage in the evolution of the debate over American colonialism. From the *émeute* of January 1893 to the annexation resolution of July 1898, the Hawaiian Islands were the source of sporadic controversy in Congress and the press. When annexation was finally consummated it came under the aegis of war, but the more fundamental arguments of the advocates of acquisition had been stated several years earlier and were quite independent of the needs of national defense in time of war. They had found clearest expression, indeed, in an article by the famous propagandist and naval historian Captain Alfred T. Mahan that appeared in March 1893: "Hawaii and Our Future Sea Power." So, too, the arguments of the unsuccessful opponents of the annexation resolution of 1898 were well rehearsed by that date. The abortive Hawaiian treaty of 1893 had alerted them to the danger: the absorption of distant peoples untutored in the ways of a self-governing republic. Expansion of this kind was without precedent; it was a false interpretation of this country's "Manifest Destiny." In an article of that title, Carl Schurz gave pungent expression to the whole range of anti-expansionist objections to the acquisition of the Hawaiian Islands.

The efforts of the Anti-Expansionists reached their climax in the great struggle over the Philippines. That battle came to dominate and overshadow the entire struggle waged between the enemies and advocates of insular expansionism. If this development lent a false impression to the chronological measurements of the debate for both contemporaries and later historians, it is nonetheless true that in many ways the question of the Philippines represented the perfect test case. More than the Samoan Islands, Hawaii, or various half-formulated projects respecting the Danish West Indies, it stood forth as a clear-cut example of the March of the Flag and the extension of the American political system to distant shores and large native populations. Four articles have been selected from the hundreds that appeared in scores of periodicals in the years 1898 through 1900. Those years saw not only a brilliant debate in the U.S. Senate but a flood of speeches, public letters, pamphlets, and essays in the public forum that exhibited a general level of intellectual coherence and literary skill perhaps never exceeded in the history of political controversy in America.

The four articles selected do not pretend to cover the full range of arguments on either side; they do reflect, however, the sense of commitment and certainty of both sides. In the articles by John Barrett, one-time American minister to Siam, and David J. Hill, Assistant Secretary of State, are exhibited the economic appeals of a career diplomat and the broader aspirations of an educator-publicist determined to convince America of its new responsibilities. In the articles of the New York divine Henry Van Dyke and the Boston municipal reformer Frank Parsons are exhibited the moral emphasis of the anti-imperialist position and the pragmatic fears of the opponents of *Realpolitik*.

The debate over Theodore Roosevelt's Panama Canal diplomacy falls beyond the boundaries of the 1890's but not beyond the boundaries of the Great Debate. The proponents of American expansion in the Pacific saw a transisthmian canal as vital to the nation's diplomatic and economic growth. Many of the defeated but unsilenced Anti-Imperialists conversely saw the diplomatic techniques of Theodore Roosevelt in Central America as furnishing proof positive of their earlier contention that imitation of European colonialism would be followed by adoption of the immoral diplomatic techniques of the Old World. Editorials of 1903 in the Boston *Daily Advertiser* and the New York *World* provide illustration of each position.

In the next section an attempt is made to illustrate further the variety of arguments of each side in the Great Debate by focusing on certain contemporary explanations respecting the stimuli and probable consequences of the expansionist movement of the 1890's. Letters of leading spokesmen and opponents of overseas expansion have been selected to give more specific demonstration of contrasting attitudes respecting the relationship of American expansion to the need for overseas markets, to the necessities of national defense, and to popular attitudes toward race and racial differences.

Letters of Albert J. Beveridge and George F. Hoar offer contrasting judgments respecting the relationship of territorial expansion and commercial growth. Letters

of Theodore Roosevelt and Edward Atkinson offer
equally divergent opinions respecting the relationship
of expansion and the military security of the republic.
No pairing of men or letters could hope to illustrate the
complexity of racial attitudes and fears among both the
proponents and enemies of expansion, but the letters of
Alfred Mahan, William James, and the Adams brothers
at least illustrate the widely variant conclusions
reached by men of the 1890's respecting the duty of
Anglo-Saxon Americans toward "less civilized peoples."

That variance is echoed with poetic exaggeration in
two much-quoted British contributions to the debate
which serve as a summary of sorts: the famous effort of
Rudyard Kipling to instruct his American cousins respecting "the White Man's Burden" and the satiric
response of another Englishman, Henry Labouchère.
These poets saw the choice facing America at the end
of the 19th century as one of crucial significance and
dramatic urgency. Was it not America's duty to "have
done with childish days," Kipling inquired. His parodist
opponent responded by asking the American people if
it was prepared to reject its heritage and "reserve for
home consumption the sacred 'rights of man.'" Such
questions were central to the argument of the opposing
sides in the controversy over the acquisition of an
island empire.

The last pair of articles, by the opposing champions
Theodore Roosevelt and William Graham Sumner, are
offered less as a conclusion than as a postscript. Perhaps the chief justification for their inclusion is that
they were the articles which first drew the attention of
the editor to the debate between the Imperialists and

the Anti-Imperialists of the 1890's. It is additionally true that there are no contemporary essays which better reflect the passion and dedication of the opposing contestants in the Great Debate.

The failure of the contestants in that debate to convince one another or to provide for a later generation the comfort of certainty does not deny the continuing importance of their effort.

America's Mission and
the Nature of Territorial Expansion

John R. Procter versus William G. Sumner

In the 1890's the *Forum* was a new addition to the list of magazines of opinion. Encouraging controversial articles on questions of public policy, it was among the first to identify expansionism — with the trusts, labor strikes, and the silver crusade — as a source of public interest and division. It published numerous articles on both sides of the debate over imperialism. Most of these pieces argued the necessity or danger of a particular acquisition, but some sought to define insular expansionism as a general policy and to place that policy in the context of the historic evolution and mission of the Republic. Two of the more successful efforts were those authored by John Robert Procter and William Graham Sumner.

John Robert Procter (1844–1903) was a southerner by birth and a geologist by training. More relevant to his public opinions, however, was his friendship with Theodore Roosevelt. It was largely as the result of Roosevelt's recommendation that Procter was appointed to the U.S. Civil Service Commission in 1893. He served on that commission for the next decade and in that period became one of the minor luminaries in the Washington circle that embraced John Hay, Henry Cabot Lodge, Henry Adams, and Captain Alfred T. Mahan. Procter shared with these men a keen interest in the power rivalries of Europe and a growing conviction that it was America's destiny to adopt a "Large Policy" respecting its international responsibilities.

William Graham Sumner (1840–1910) was a scholar by training, a professor by choice, and a publicist by temperament. A member of the Yale University faculty from 1872 to 1910, he is best known as an apostle of Social Darwinism, a defender of a governmental policy of laissez-faire. Though it is true that Sumner was convinced that governmental interference in the operations of the economy could be neither scientific nor intelligent, he was no unthinking champion of big business and industrial combination. He was rather an independent-minded scholar inspired by strong moral convictions and convinced that the professor's lectern should face the public as well as the classroom. From that lectern he addressed himself to the issues of free trade, civil service reform, hard money, and diplomatic consistency. On the latter count he saw imperialism as a policy false to the history and promise of the American Republic.

1. Isolation or Imperialism

JOHN R. PROCTER

The year 1898 will be one of the epoch-marking years in the history of the United States. In this year is to be decided the great question of whether this country is to continue in its policy of political isolation, or is to take its rightful place among the great World-Powers, and assume the unselfish obligations and responsibilities demanded by the enlightened civilization of the age.

Many of our statesmen, forgetting that *prestige* is as dear to nations as to individuals, and underestimating the inherited racial instincts, the restless activities, and the aggressive enterprise of our people, wrongly imagine that they can remain contented with political and commercial isolation, and satisfied, as are the Chinese, to be guided in questions of immediate and world-wide importance by quotations from obsolete texts from the wise sayings of remote ancestors.

When Washington wrote his justly celebrated Farewell Address, nations were as distant from each other in time, and communication was as slow and difficult, as at the beginning of the Christian era; but steam and electricity have so drawn the ends of the earth together that civilized society is fast becoming one highly organized and interdependent whole.

Each generation has the power to shape its own destinies; and had Washington and his fellow-patriots been governed by warnings against a departure from traditions, our present form of government would never have been established, the Constitution would have been rejected by the States, and untold evils would have resulted. . . .

In answer to the arguments that there is no constitutional provision for governing acquired territory, it is only necessary to quote from Section 3, Art. IV of the Constitution:

Originally published in the *Forum*, Vol. XXVI (September 1898), pp. 14–26.

The Congress shall have power to dispose of and make all needful rules and regulations respecting the territory or other property belonging to the United States.

This country has acquired territory by purchase, by conquest, by treaty, and has made such laws for the government of such acquired territory as seemed most suitable to the requirements. There is no constitutional bar to this country having colonies or dependencies corresponding to the Crown colonies of Great Britain, or to the self-governing colonies, such as New Zealand and Natal. . . .

The world has been divided into two opposing colonial systems: (1) the Continental European, or government of provinces or dependencies from the central or home government — acquiring colonies for the advantage supposed to accrue from the monopoly of their commerce; and (2) the Anglo-American system, where the government is the creature of the union of previously autonomous parts, as in the United States and Canada, where colonies are encouraged to establish local self-government, and where colonies such as the English Crown colonies are thrown open to unrestricted trade. We thus have two antagonistic systems and forces contending for world-supremacy. Continental Europe inherited from Rome the system of governing colonies for the exclusive benefit of the home governments; while the Anglo-Americans have developed their systems from the germs inherited from their Teutonic ancestors of Northern Europe. . . .

In this epoch-marking year of 1898 the remaining vestige of the Roman system of colonial government is to be driven from the western hemisphere; descendants of the Norse sea-rovers are to carry the victorious banner of our civilization to the confines of the Far East; and there, in conjunction with their kinsmen from Britain, they are to settle for all time the question whether the repressive militarism of the Middle Ages shall be extended over more than one-half of the population of the globe. It is the old contest of the centuries

transferred to another field of action. On one side are represented the Powers of Continental Europe, striving to obtain
concessions, looking to the acquisition of possessions in the
Far East, with the intention of closing the ports of such
acquired territories to the commerce of the world, by the
placing of high customs duties on all imports other than those
from the country in control. On the other, Great Britain and
the United States, being enabled by their resources, the industry and inventiveness of their peoples, and their facilities
for reaching foreign markets to compete on equal terms, — and
having a large and increasing population dependent on foreign
markets in which to dispose of an increasing surplus production, — their interests demand that no combination of Powers
be allowed to close the ports of Asia to their commerce.

Hitherto the United States has lent no aid to England in
her efforts to avert the impending danger. Fettered by its
policy of isolation, this country has been strangely remiss in
asserting its rights and guarding its interests. . . .

Why, but for our isolation paralysis, do we not unite with
Great Britain in safeguarding the interests of our people in
China and in other countries of Asia? Our fathers met the
"Family Compact" of 1761 and the Holy Alliance in 1823
when they were comparatively weak; and now that we are
rich and powerful, we should not hesitate to meet, if necessary, a "Concert of the Powers."

. . . . .

Notwithstanding the vast naval preparation of [Germany,
Russia, and France] . . . it is fated that Anglo-American descendants of the mighty seamen whose glorious achievements
are the common heritage of our race must ever hold dominion
over the seas; provided there is mutual aid and cooperation.
The insular position of the United States and the British
possessions renders large standing armies unnecessary, so
long as these two countries are on friendly terms and maintain command of the seas. . . .

With just and wise administration, colonial possessions are a source of strength rather than of weakness. The designs of the Powers in the Far East, if successful, will deprive this country of an already large market, which must increase to enormous proportions in the near future, and, by depriving Great Britain of her best market will lessen the ability of our best customer to purchase our products. Last year Great Britain purchased our products to the value of $483,625,024; and she and her colonies took 60 per cent of the total value of our exports to all the world. The value of the trade of Great Britain and the United States with China amounts to six times that of the combined trade of Germany, France, and Russia with the Celestial Empire; consequently, England and the United States have a right to declare that their interests in China are paramount, and to act in concert in safeguarding those interests. China, the United States, and the British possessions have the largest extent of coast-line fronting on the Pacific, with a growing community of interests. Great Britain has secured the important naval stations of Hong Kong and Wei-hai-wei for the protection of her large interests; and she has a large and efficient auxiliary force conveniently near in India.

Fortunately, we can have at Manila a most advantageous distributing-point for our commerce, as well as a naval base of great strategic importance. By good government and just administration, the natives of the Philippines can be made a prosperous people, and, under the discipline and leadership of American officers, an effective fighting-force, if necessary. . . . So long as Great Britain holds Gibraltar, Aden, Cape Town, and the Falkland Islands, and the United States controls Hawaii, the Philippines, and the canal route connecting the Atlantic with the Pacific, these two Powers can dominate the Pacific and Indian oceans.

Our race has two important characteristics, as has been well shown by Mr. Kidd in his "Social Evolution": (1) the highly developed power of individual initiative, and (2) what he has well termed social efficiency. The Tropics are peopled with millions of low social efficiency; and it seems to be the fate of the black and yellow races to have their countries parcelled out and administered by efficient races from the Temperate Zone. If such administration be just, wise, and humane, like the administration of Lord Cromer in Egypt, it will be for the upbuilding and enlightenment of the peoples of the Tropics, and the advance of the blessings of civilization over the world.

The world's future depends largely on the decision which we are about to render as to the policy of this country in relation to the great problems now confronting us. If America is henceforth to be one of the determining factors in advancing and defending the principles of Anglo-Saxon civilization throughout the world, the dangers which threaten that civilization will disappear like the mists of the morning. Already some of the good effects of the abandonment of our policy of isolation are apparent, both at home and abroad. Introspection in nations, as in individuals, is frequently an evidence of disease; and it is questionable whether the political isolation of this country, and the consequent narrowing of our political horizon, may not have been a cause of the unrest and internal dissensions which have been so notable during recent years, and which have brought to the front the purveyors of political quack cure-alls for imagined as well as apparent evils. Provincialism and parochial politics have in many localities foisted inferior men into places of public trust. Since we have, by recent events, been forced to face wider responsibilities and a broadening field of action, some of the evils with which the country was supposed to be afflicted have vanished. . . .

In the interests of civilization and humanity, this country should retain the Philippines. Then the chain of islands extending along the entire eastern coast-line of Asia will be owned by Japan, the United States, Great Britain, and the Netherlands—all seafaring nations, and countries having like interests to guard. . . . The interests of peace and progress demand that this country should accept the responsibilities thrust upon it by Dewey's glorious victory at Manila. Wherever our flag shall be planted, let it remain and carry freedom from oppression. But we should not forget that peoples who have for centuries been subjected to misrule and oppression have yet to learn the principles of self-government. Let us avoid the criminal blunder made in the past, when we bestowed with unthinking liberality the highest privilege of Anglo-Saxon freedom upon an illiterate, alien race just emerging from bondage, — a priceless privilege which our fathers attained only through centuries of patient self-development, — and thus prevented the placing of the rights of suffrage upon an educational basis applicable to whites and blacks alike. . . .

Our administrators have now an opportunity to achieve the most momentous results in broad statesmanship ever vouchsafed to the rulers of any age or country. . . . From the blood of our heroes, shed at Santiago and Manila, there shall arise a New Imperialism, replacing the waning Imperialism of Old Rome; an Imperialism destined to carry world-wide the principles of Anglo-Saxon peace and justice, liberty and law.

2. The Fallacy of Territorial Extension

WILLIAM GRAHAM SUMNER

The traditional belief is that a state aggrandizes itself by territorial extension, so that winning new land is gaining in wealth and prosperity, just as an individual would gain if he increased his land possessions. It is undoubtedly true that a state may be so small in territory and population that it cannot serve the true purposes of a state for its citizens, especially in international relations with neighboring states

Originally published in the *Forum*, Vol. XXI (June 1896), pp. 414– 19.

which control a large aggregate of men and capital. There is, therefore, under given circumstances, a size of territory and population which is at the maximum of advantage for the civil unit. The unification of Germany and Italy was apparently advantageous for the people affected. . . . The opinion may be risked, however, that Russia has carried out a policy of territorial extension which has been harmful to its internal integration. For three hundred years it has been reaching out after more territory, and has sought the grandeur and glory of conquest and size. To this it has sacrificed the elements of social and industrial strength. The autocracy has been confirmed and established because it is the only institution which symbolizes and maintains the unity of the great mass, and the military and tax burdens have distorted the growth of the society to such an extent as to produce disease and weakness.

Territorial aggrandizement enhances the glory and personal importance of the man who is the head of a dynastic state. The fallacy of confusing this with the greatness and strength of the state itself is an open pitfall close at hand. It might seem that a republic, one of whose chief claims to superiority over a monarchy lies in avoiding the danger of confusing the king with the state, ought to be free from this fallacy of national greatness, but we have plenty of examples to prove that the traditional notions are not cut off by changing names and forms.

The notion that gain of territory is gain of wealth and strength for the state, after the expedient size has been won, is a delusion. In the Middle Ages the beneficial interest in land and the jurisdiction over the people who lived on it were united in one person. The modern great states, upon their formation, took to themselves the jurisdiction, and the beneficial interest turned into full property in land. The confusion of the two often reappears now, and it is one of the most fruitful causes of fallacy in public questions. It is often said that the United States owns silver mines, and it is inferred that the policy of the state in regard to money and currency ought to be controlled in some way by this fact. The "United States" as a subject of property rights and of monetary claims . . . may be best defined by calling it the "Fiscus." This legal person owns no silver mines. . . . The beneficial and property interest in the mines belongs to individuals, and they win profits only by conducting the exploitation of the mines with an expenditure of labor and capital. These individuals are of many nationalities. They alone own the product and have the use and enjoyment of it. . . .

It is said that the boundary between Alaska and British America runs through a gold field, and some people are in great anxiety as to who will "grab" it. If an American can go over to the English side and mine gold there for his profit, under English laws and jurisdiction, and an Englishman can come over to the American side and mine gold there for his profit, under American laws and jurisdiction, what difference does it make where the line falls? . . .

If the United States should admit Hawaii to the Union, the Fiscus of the former state would collect more taxes and incur more expenses. The circumstances are such that the latter would probably be the greater. The United States would not acquire a square foot of land in property, unless it paid for it. Individual Americans would get no land to till, without paying for it, and would win no products from it except by wisely expending their labor and capital on it. All that, they can do now. So long as there is a government on the islands, native or other, which is competent to guarantee peace, order, and security, no more is necessary, and for any outside power to seize the jurisdiction is an unjustifiable aggression. . . . The jurisdiction would, in any case, be a burden, and any state might be glad to see any other state assume the burden. . . . The best case is, therefore, always that in which the resident population produce their own state by the institutions of self-government.

What private individuals want is free access, under order

and security, to any part of the earth's surface, in order that they may avail themselves of its natural resources for their use, either by investment or commerce. If, therefore, we could have free trade with Hawaii while somebody else had the jurisdiction, we should gain all the advantages and escape all the burdens. The Constitution of the United States establishes absolute free trade between all parts of the territory under its jurisdiction. A large part of our population were thrown into indignant passion because the [Cleveland] Administration rejected the annexation of Hawaii, regarding it like the act of a man who refuses the gift of a farm. These persons were generally those who are thrown into excitement by any proposition of free trade. They will not, therefore, accept free trade with the islands while somebody else has the trouble and burden of the jurisdiction, but they would accept free trade with the islands eagerly if they could get the burden of the jurisdiction too. . . .

The island of Cuba may fall into anarchy. If it does, the civilized world may look to the United States to take the jurisdiction and establish order and security there. We might be compelled to do it. It would, however, be a great burden, and possibly a fatal calamity to us. Probably any proposition that England should take it would call out a burst of jingo passion against which all reasoning would be powerless. We ought to pray that England would take it. . . . If we take the jurisdiction of the island, we shall find ourselves in a political dilemma, each horn of which is as disastrous as the other; either we must govern it as a subject province, or we must admit it into the Union as a State or group of States. Our system is unfit for the government of subject provinces. They have no place in it. They would become seats of corruption, which would react on our own body politic. If we admitted the island as a State or group of States, we should have to let it help govern us. The prospect of adding to the present Senate a number of Cuban senators, either native or carpet-bag, is one of whose terrors it is not necessary to unfold.

Nevertheless it appears that there is a large party which would not listen to free trade with the island while any other nation has the jurisdiction of it, but who are ready to grab it at any cost, and to take free trade with it, provided that they can get the political burdens too.

This confederated state of ours was never planned for indefinite expansion, or for an imperial policy. We boast of it a great deal, but we must know that its advantages are won at the cost of its limitations, as is the case with most things in the world. The Fathers of the Republic planned a confederation of free and peaceful industrial commonwealths, shielded by their geographical position from the jealousies, rivalries, and traditional jealousies of the Old World, and bringing all the resources of civilization to bear for the domestic happiness of the population only. They meant to have no grand statecraft, or "high politics"; no "balance of power" or "reasons of state," which had cost the human race so much. They meant to offer no field for what Benjamin Franklin called the "pest of glory." It is the limitation of this scheme of the state that the state created under it must forego a great number of the grand functions of European states; especially that it contains no methods and apparatus of conquest, extension, domination, and imperialism. The plan of the Fathers would have no controlling authority for us, if it had been proved by experience that that plan was narrow, inadequate, and mistaken. Are we prepared to vote that it has proved so? For our territorial extension has reached limits which are complete for all purposes and leave no necessity for "rectification of boundaries." Any extension will open questions; not close them. Any extension will not make us more secure where we are, but will force us to take new measures to secure our new acquisitions. The preservation of acquisitions will force us to reorganize our internal resources, so as to make it possible to prepare them in advance and to mobilize them with promptitude. This will lessen liberty and require discipline. It will increase taxation and all the pressure of government. It will divert the national energy from the provision of self-maintenance and comfort for the people, and will necessitate stronger and more elaborate governmental machinery. All this will be disastrous to republican institutions and to democracy. Moreover all extension puts a new strain on the internal cohesion of the pre-existing mass, threatening a new cleavage within. . . .

The sum of the matter is that colonization and territorial extension are burdens, not gains. . . .

The Samoan Protectorate and
the Debate Foreshadowed

New York Tribune *versus Springfield* Republican

Although the revival of interest in overseas expansion in the last dozen years of the 19th century is
susceptible to rational explanation, its first fruit was
largely the result of accident. Darwinian theory, surplus
production, the end of the frontier, the force of imitation, the wish for distraction from internal problems,
the revival of the tradition of Manifest Destiny may in
combination provide the ingredients for a satisfactory
historical analysis respecting the revival of expansionist
sentiment. They do not explain why the first if limited
accomplishment of American imperialism occurred in a
tiny archipelago of the South Pacific.

There had been indications of American interest in
the Samoan Islands before 1889, and indeed a treaty of
sorts signed in 1878 with a Samoan chief which indicated the concern of the U.S. navy in obtaining a
coaling station at Pago Pago, but few were the Americans who identified the Samoan Islands with the laws
of progress or the needs of economic expansion. There

was more of chance than of plan in the development of a minor international crisis in the Samoan archipelago that eventuated in the establishment of a tripartite protectorate and the subsequent division of that archipelago between Germany and the United States.

In the years 1887 to 1889, the internal quarrels of the Samoan natives were matched by the suspicions and intrigues of the consular representatives of Germany, Great Britain, and the United States in the harbors of Pago Pago and Apia. It would appear that the plots and ambitions of the American representative were more personal than official in inspiration, and the interest of Washington was occasioned more by a suspicion of Germany than a hunger for the Samoas. Foreshadowing the rising jingoism of the next decade, however, was the readiness of a few American papers to associate the frustration of Germany with the naval strength of the United States.

The farcical but potentially dangerous "furor consularis" in Samoa was eventually dampened by the agreement of the three home governments to arrange a conference at Berlin. It was there that the temporary tripartite protectorate was arranged and Washington's "great rule of conduct" modestly sabotaged.

Reaction in the American press was limited in coverage and depth of conviction. Whitelaw Reid (1837–1912) of the New York *Tribune* and Samuel Bowles, Jr. (1851–1915) of the Springfield *Republican* were among the few who saw in American involvement in the Samoan imbroglio the possible beginnings of a new departure for American diplomacy. They viewed the prospect with respective pleasure and alarm, and

their contrary opinions serve to introduce the debate
between the advocates and opponents of overseas expansion.

3. The View of an Expansionist Editor

WHITELAW REID

A CAMPAIGN OF CONQUEST

From the New York Tribune, *February 1, 1889.*

Germany has entered upon a campaign of conquest in
Samoa. . . . Prince Bismarck's proposal for a renewal of the
conference is only a convenient method of throwing dust in
the eyes of Secretary Bayard, who has been his credulous
dupe for four years. . . . Why should the United States be
drawn into another conference when the conditions under
which the last one was held were wantonly violated by both
Germany and England? . . .

Two courses are open to the United States. One is a policy
of action with the risk which it involves. The other is a policy
of inaction with whatever apparent discredit attends it. Germany has every intention of securing absolute control of
Samoa. It has become a commercial depot in the South Seas,
and occupies a central position in Prince Bismarck's scheme
of colonial enterprise. Samoa is to be the collecting and dis-
tributing point for German commerce in the South Seas, and
will be a dependency of the Empire unless the United States
is prepared and anxious to intervene with vigor and determination. Diplomatic expedients such as the proposed conference will be of no avail. It is Congress that is now armed with
full responsibility for deciding whether German usurpation is
to be challenged or condoned. Are we enough concerned

[with these disputes, five thousand miles from our present frontier,] to take one step that is not actually compelled by National self-respect?

4. The View of One Opposed

SAMUEL BOWLES, JR.

OUR SAMOAN POLICY

From the Springfield Republican, *January 12, 1889.*

. . . The wise advice to keep out of entangling alliances may well be heeded in the Samoan complications. We have a coaling station and enjoy commercial privileges on those islands, and it may be a matter of regret that the aim of Germany is evidently to gain complete supremacy there, but nothing short of rank jingoism will lead us to go one step beyond the technical protection of our interests. Greenbaum [the American consul] was not authorized to protect anything but American life and property; nor are we justified by the true foreign policy that becomes a republic to send a fleet into the heart of Oceanica and intermediate in an affair between two native kings because in our opinion one of them is not receiving fair treatment at the hands of Germany.

Hawaii and the Debate Begun

Alfred T. Mahan versus Carl Schurz

The dispute over the annexation of the Hawaiian Islands falls into two clearly separated time periods reaching their particular heights in 1893 and 1898. Annexation was only consummated with the Spanish-American War, but the arguments that were offered for and against the annexation resolution of July 1898 had been earlier articulated by advocates and opponents of the abortive annexation effort of 1893. In that earlier debate the most searching analyses of the advantages and dangers of annexation had been offered, respectively, by the publicist of Sea Power, Captain Alfred Thayer Mahan, and the political moralist and maverick, Carl Schurz.

Alfred Thayer Mahan (1840–1914) was a career naval officer who found avocation and recognition in the study of history. He was called to lecture on naval tactics and history at the newly established War College at Newport, Rhode Island, in 1886, and published a revised version of those lectures in 1890 under the title *The Influence of Sea Power upon History, 1660–1783*. The impact of that book and its successors

on the diplomatic goals and naval construction pro-
grams of the United States and other Western nations
has perhaps been exaggerated, but that Mahan was one
of the few historians to have direct influence on the
policy makers of his own time is not to be denied.

It was Mahan's contention that history proved that
Sea Power was essential to the military security and the
growth and vitality of a nation. Control of essential
trade lanes as well as contiguous waters was vital to
American power and prosperity. Mahan called for an
enlarged navy and merchant marine, an isthmian canal,
and the acquisition of island colonies that could serve
as naval bases and as vestibules for an expanding foreign trade. The annexation of the Hawaiian Islands was
a necessary beginning.

Carl Schurz (1829–1906) lived, wrote, and died as a
dissident. The best known of the refugee *émigrés* of
1848 to come to America, he quickly established himself as a leader of the German-American community
and as an orator and writer of persuasive eloquence in
his newly adopted language. A Union general and
friend of Lincoln, Schurz served a single term after the
war as a senator from Missouri and then as Secretary
of the Interior in Hayes's Administration. His natural
residence, however, was not in office but in opposition.
He was the greatest of the Mugwumps — that band of
self-righteous champions of political rectitude and cau-
tion. If occasionally inconsistent in his attacks on the
domestic policies of his opponents, he was undeviating
in his belief that America should keep aloof from foreign entanglements. In Schurz's eyes the mission of
America demanded that she serve as a beacon of hope
for the oppressed peoples of the world, and to sustain

her proper image she must maintain her isolation from
the corrupting ambitions of European monarchies. The
ideal of America was peace, not power; a policy of
colonial expansion would sacrifice her unique position
and degrade her standing before the bar of world opinion.

5. Hawaii and Our Future Sea-Power

ALFRED T. MAHAN

The suddenness — so far, at least, as the general public is
concerned — with which the long-existing troubles in Hawaii
have come to a head, and the character of the advances
reported to be addressed to the United States by the revolutionary government, formally recognized as *de facto* by our
representative on the spot, add another to the many significant instances furnished by history that, as men in the midst
of life are in death, so nations in the midst of peace find
themselves confronted with unexpected causes of dissension,
conflicts of interests, whose results may be, on the one hand,
war, or, on the other, abandonment of clear and imperative
national advantage in order to avoid an issue for which preparation has not been made. By no premeditated contrivance
of our own, by the cooperation of a series of events which,
however dependent step by step upon human action, were not
intended to prepare the present crisis, the United States finds
herself compelled to answer a question — to make a decision — not unlike and not less momentous than that required
of the Roman senate when the Mamertine garrison invited it
to occupy Messina and so to abandon the hitherto traditional

Originally published in the *Forum*, Vol. XV (March, 1893), pp. 1–11.

policy which had confined the expansion of Rome to the Italian peninsula. For let it not be over-looked that, whether we wish or no, we *must* answer the question, we *must* make the decision. The issue cannot be dodged. Absolute inaction in such a case is a decision as truly as the most vehement action. We can now advance, but, the conditions of the world being what they are, if we do not advance we recede; for there is involved not so much a particular action as a question of principle pregnant of great consequences in one direction or in the other.

Occasion of serious difficulty should not, indeed, here arise. . . . Arrested on the south by the rights of a race wholly alien to us, and on the north by a body of states of like traditions to our own, whose freedom to choose their own affiliations we respect, we have come to the sea. In our infancy we bordered upon the Atlantic only; our youth carried our boundary to the Gulf of Mexico; to-day maturity sees us upon the Pacific. Have we no right or no call to progress farther in any direction? Are there for us beyond the sea-horizon none of those essential interests, of those evident dangers, which impose a policy and confer rights?

This is the question that has long been looming upon the brow of a future now rapidly passing into the present. Of it the Hawaiian incident is a part—intrinsically, perhaps, a small part—but in its relations to the whole so vital that, as has before been said, a wrong decision does not stand by itself, but involves, not only in principle but in fact, recession along the whole line. . . .

. . . . .

The military or strategic value of a naval position depends upon its situation, upon its strength, and upon its resources. Of the three, the first is of most consequence, because it results from the nature of things; whereas the two latter, when deficient, can be artificially supplied, in whole or in part. Fortifications remedy the weaknesses of a position, foresight accumulates beforehand the resources which nature does not yield on the spot; but it is not within the power of man to change the geographical situation of a point which lies outside the limit of strategic effect. . . . While in itself the ocean opposes no obstacle to a vessel taking any one of the numerous routes that can be traced upon the surface of the globe between two points, conditions of distance or convenience, of traffic or of wind, do prescribe certain usual courses. Where these pass near an ocean position, still more where they use it, it has an influence over them, and where several routes cross near by that influence becomes very great — is commanding.

Let us now apply these considerations to the Hawaiian group. To any one viewing a map that shows the full extent of the Pacific Ocean, with its shores on either side, two circumstances will be strikingly and immediately apparent. He will see at a glance that the Sandwich Islands stand by themselves, in a state of comparative isolation, amid a vast expanse of sea; and, again, that they form the centre of a large circle whose radius is approximately — and very closely — the distance from Honolulu to San Francisco. . . . The distance from San Francisco to Honolulu, twenty-one hundred miles — easy steaming distance — is substantially the same as that from Honolulu to the Gilbert, Marshall, Samoan, Society, and Marquesas groups, all under European control, except Samoa, in which we have a part influence.

To have a central position such as this, and to be alone, having no rival and admitting no alternative throughout an extensive tract, are conditions that at once fix the attention of the strategist — it may be added, of the statesmen of commerce likewise. But to this striking combination is to be added the remarkable relations borne by these singularly placed islands to the greater commercial routes traversing this vast expanse known to us as the Pacific — not only, however, to those now actually in use, important as they are, but also to those that must necessarily be called into being by that future to which the Hawaiian incident compels our too willing attention. Circumstances, as was before tritely remarked, create centres, between which communication necessarily follows; and in the vista of the future all, however dimly, discern a new and great centre that must greatly modify existing sea-routes, as well as bring new ones into existence. Whether the canal of the Central American isthmus be eventually at Panama or at Nicaragua matters little to the question now in hand. . . . Whichever it be, the convergence there of so many ships from the Atlantic and the Pacific will constitute a centre of commerce, interoceanic and inferior to few, if to any, in the world; one whose approaches will be jealously watched and whose relations to the other centres of the Pacific by the lines joining it to them must be carefully examined. Such study of the commercial routes and their relations to the Hawaiian Islands, taken together with the other strategic considerations previously set forth, completes the synopsis of facts which determine the value of the group for conferring either commercial or naval control. . . .

. . . . .

From the foregoing considerations may be inferred the importance of the Hawaiian Islands as a position powerfully influencing the commercial and military control of the Pacific, and especially of the northern Pacific, in which the United States, geographically, has the strongest right to assert herself. These are the main advantages, which can be termed positive: those, namely, which directly advance commercial security and naval control. To the negative advantages of possession, by removing conditions which, if the islands were in the hands of any other power, would constitute to us disadvantages and threats, allusion only will be made. The serious menace to our Pacific coast and our Pacific trade, if so important a position were held by a possible enemy, has been frequently mentioned in the press and dwelt upon in the diplomatic papers which are from time to time given to the

public. It may be assumed that it is generally acknowledged.
Upon one particular, however, too much stress cannot be
laid, one to which naval officers cannot but be more sensitive
than the general public, and that is the immense disadvantage
to us of any maritime enemy having a coaling-station well
within twenty-five hundred miles, as this is, of every point of
our coastline from Puget Sound to Mexico. Were there many
others available we might find it difficult to exclude from all.
There is, however, but the one. Shut out from the Sandwich
Islands as a coal base, an enemy is thrown back for supplies
of fuel to distances of thirty-five hundred or four thousand
miles—or between seven thousand and eight thousand, going
and coming—an impediment to sustained maritime operations
well-nigh prohibitive. . . . It is rarely that so important a fac-
tor in the attack or defence of a coastline—of a
sea-frontier—is concentrated in a single position, and the
circumstance renders doubly imperative upon us to secure it,
if we righteously can.

It is to be hoped, also, that the opportunity thus thrust
upon us may not be narrowly viewed, as though it concerned
but one section of our country or one portion of its external
trade or influence. This is no mere question of a particular
act, for which, possibly, just occasion may not yet have
offered; but of a principle, a policy, fruitful of many future
acts, to enter upon which, in the fulness of our national
progress, the time has now arrived. The principle accepted, to
be conditioned only by a just and candid regard for the rights
and reasonable susceptibilities of other nations—none of
which is contravened by the step here immediately under
discussion—the annexation, even, of Hawaii would be no
mere sporadic effort, irrational because disconnected from an
adequate motive, but a first-fruit and a token that the nation
in its evolution has aroused itself to the necessity of carrying
its life—that has been the happiness of those under its
influence—beyond the borders that have heretofore sufficed
for its activities. That the vaunted blessings of our economy

are not to be forced upon the unwilling may be conceded; but the concession does not deny the right nor the wisdom of gathering in those who wish to come. Comparative religion teaches that creeds which reject missionary enterprise are foredoomed to decay. May it not be so with nations? Certainly the glorious record of England is consequent mainly upon the spirit and traceable to the time when she launched out into the deep — without formulated policy, it is true, or foreseeing the future to which her star was leading, but obeying the instinct which in the infancy of nations anticipates the more reasoned impulses of experience. Let us, too, learn from her experience. Not all at once did England become the great sea power which she is, but step by step, as opportunity offered, she has moved on to the world-wide preeminence now held by English speech and by institutions sprung from English germs. How much poorer would the world have been had Englishmen heeded the cautious hesitancy that now bids us reject every advance beyond our shore-lines! And can any one doubt that a cordial, if unformulated, understanding between the two chief states of English tradition, to spread freely, without mutual jealousy and in mutual support, would greatly increase the world's sum of happiness?

But if a plea of the world's welfare seem suspiciously like a cloak for national self-interest, let the latter be frankly accepted as the adequate motive which it assuredly is. Let us not shrink from pitting a broad self-interest against the narrow self-interest to which some would restrict us. The demands of our three great sea-boards, the Atlantic, the Gulf, and the Pacific — each for itself, and all for the strength that comes from drawing closer the ties between them — are calling for the extension, through the Isthmian Canal, of that broad sea-common along which, and along which alone, in all the ages prosperity has moved. Land-carriage, always restricted and therefore always slow, toils enviously but hopelessly behind, vainly seeking to replace and supplant the royal highway of Nature's own making. Corporate interests, vigorous in that power of concentration which is the strength of armies and of minorities, may here for a while withstand the ill-organized strivings of the multitude, only dimly conscious of its wants; yet the latter, however temporarily opposed and baffled, is sure at last, like the blind forces of nature, to overwhelm all that stand in the way of its necessary progress. So the Isthmian Canal is an inevitable part in the future of the United States; yet scarcely an integral part, for it cannot be separated from other necessary incidents of a policy dependent upon it, whose details cannot be exactly foreseen. But because the precise steps that may hereafter be opportune or necessary cannot yet be certainly foretold, is not a reason the less, but a reason the more, for establishing a principle of action which may serve to guide as opportunities arise. Let us start from the fundamental truth, warranted by history, that control of the seas, and especially along the great lines drawn by national interest or national commerce, is the chief among the merely material elements in the power and prosperity of nations. It is so because the sea is the world's great medium of circulation. From this necessarily follows the principle that, as subsidiary to such control, it is imperative to take possession, when it can righteously be done, of such maritime positions as contribute to secure command. If this principle be adopted, there will be no hesitation about taking the positions—and they are many—upon the approaches to the Isthmus, whose interests incline them to seek us. It has its application also to the present case of Hawaii. . . .

6. "Manifest Destiny"

CARL SCHURZ

Whenever there is a project on foot to annex foreign territory to this republic the cry of "manifest destiny" is raised to produce the impression that all opposition to such a project is a struggle against fate. Forty years ago this cry had a peculiar significance. The slave-holders saw in the rapid growth of the free States a menace to the existence of slavery. In order to strengthen themselves in Congress they needed more slave States, and looked therefore to the acquisition of foreign territory on which slavery existed — in the first place, the island of Cuba. . . . There was still another force behind the demand for territorial expansion. It consisted in the youthful optimism at that time still inspiring the minds of many Americans with the idea that this republic, being charged with the mission of being the banner of freedom over the whole civilized world, could transform any country, inhabited by any kind of population, into something like itself simply by extending over it the magic charm of its political institutions. Such sentiments had been strengthened by the revolutionary movements of 1848 in Europe, which invited a comparison between American and European conditions, and stimulated in the American a feeling of assured superiority, as well as of generous sympathy with other less-favored nations. . . . It was, however, the Southern "manifest-destiny" movement, with a strong organized interest behind it and well defined purposes in view, that exercised the greater influence upon the politics of the country. . . .

The civil war weakened the demand for territorial expansion in two ways. With the abolition of slavery the powerful interest which had stood behind the annexation policy

Originally published in *Harper's New Monthly Magazine*, Vol. LXXXVII (October 1893), pp. 737–46.

disappeared forever. And as to the sentimental movement, the great crisis which brought the Union so near to destruction rudely staggered the jubilant Fourth-of-July optimism of former days and reminded the American people of the inherent inadequateness of mere political institutions to the solution of all problems of human society.... A healthy scepticism took the place of youthful over-confidence. It stimulated earnest inquiry into existing conditions, and brought forth a strong feeling among our people that we should rather make sure of what we had, and improve it, than throw our energies into fanciful foreign ventures.

Only very few of the public men of the time still delighted in "manifest destiny" dreams....

.....

The recent attempt made by President Harrison to precipitate the Hawaiian Islands into our Union has again stirred up the public interest in the matter of territorial expansion, and called forth the cry of "manifest destiny" once more....

The new "manifest destiny" precept means, in point of principle, not merely the incorporation in the United States of territory contiguous to our borders, but rather the acquisition of such territory, far and near, as may be useful in enlarging our commercial advantages, and in securing to our navy facilities desirable for the operations of a great naval power. Aside from the partisan declaimers whose interest in the matter is only that of political effect, this policy finds favor with several not numerically strong but very demonstrative classes of people: Americans who have business ventures in foreign lands, or who wish to embark in such; citizens of an ardent national ambition who think that the conservative traditions of our foreign policy are out of date, and that it is time for the United States to take an active part and to assert their power in the international politics of the world, and to this end to avail themselves of every chance for territorial aggrandizement; and lastly, what may be called the navy in-

terest — officers of the navy and others taking especial pride in
the development of our naval force, many of whom advocate
a large increase of our war-fleet to support a vigorous foreign
policy, and a vigorous foreign policy to give congenial occupation and to secure further increase to our war-fleet. These
forces we find bent upon exciting the ambition of the American people whenever a chance for the acquisition of foreign
territory heaves in sight.

As to the first of these classes, it is certainly not to be
denied that among the American-adventurers in foreign parts
there are many respectable characters, whose interests are
entitled to consideration, and may be, under certain circumstances, entitled also to active protection by our government.
But when they ask, under whatever pretext, that for the
advancement or protection of their interests the countries in
which they are engaged in private business should be incorporated in this republic, the apparent patriotism of their
demand should be received with due distrust. . . .

The patriotic ardor of those who would urge this republic
into the course of indiscriminate territorial aggrandizement to
make it the greatest of the great powers of the world deserves
more serious consideration. To see his country powerful and
respected among the nations of the earth, and to secure to it
all those advantages to which its character and position en-
title it, is the natural desire of every American. In this sentiment we are all agreed. There may, however, be grave
differences of opinion as to how this end can be most surely,
most completely, and most worthily maintained. This is not a
mere matter of patriotic sentiment but a problem of statesmanship. No conscientious citizen will think a moment of
incorporating a single square mile of foreign soil in this Union
without most earnestly considering how it will be likely to
affect our social and political condition at home as well as our
relations with the world abroad.

According to the spirit of our constitutional system, foreign
territory should be acquired only with a view to its admission,

at no very distant day, into this Union as one or more States on an equal footing with the other States. The population inhabiting such territory, and admitted into the union with it, would have to be endowed with certain rights and powers, and the United States would have to undertake certain obligations with regard to them. The people of the new States would not only govern themselves as to their home concerns, but also take part in the government of the whole country. . . . This republic would admit them as equal members to its national household, to its family circle, and take upon itself all the responsibilities for them which this admission involves. To do this safely it would have to act with keen discrimination. . . .

. . . . .

The consequences which inevitably would follow the acquisition of Cuba, which is especially alluring to the annexationist, may serve as an example. Cuba, so they tell us, possesses rich natural resources worth having. It is in the hands of a European power that may, under certain circumstances, become hostile to us. It is only a few miles from the coast of Florida. It "threatens" that coast. It "commands" also the Gulf of Mexico, with the mouths of the Mississippi and the Caribbean Sea. Its population is discontented; it wishes to cut loose from Spain and join us. If we do not take Cuba "some other power will take it." That power may be hostile. Let us take it ourselves. What then? Santo Domingo is only a few miles distant from Cuba; also a country of rich resources; other powers several times tried to get it; if in the hands of a hostile power it would "threaten" Cuba; it also "commands" the Caribbean Sea. . . . To acquire the Haitian Republic we shall have to fight; it will cost men and money, but we can easily beat the negroes. . . . Puerto Rico will come as a matter of course with Cuba. The British possessions of Jamaica will still be there to "threaten" and "command" everything else. It will be difficult to get it and the other little islands from the clutch of the British lion. Thus all the more necessary will it be to have possession of the mainland bordering and "commanding" the Gulf of Mexico and the Caribbean Sea on the western side. We must have all the "keys" to the seas and to the land, or at least as many as we can possibly get, one to protect another. In fact, when once well launched on this course, we shall hardly find a stopping-place north of the Gulf of Darien; and we shall have an abundance of reasons, one as good as another, for not stopping even there. . . .

Imagine now fifteen or twenty, or even more, States inhabited by a people so utterly different from ours in origin, in customs and habits, in traditions, language, morals, impulses, ways of thinking — in almost everything that constitutes social and political life — and these people remaining under the climatic influences which in a great measure have made them what they are, and render an essential change of their character impossible — imagine a large number of such States to form part of this Union, and through dozens of Senators and scores of Representatives in Congress, and millions of votes in our Presidential elections, to participate in making our laws, in filling the executive places of our government, and in impressing themselves upon the spirit of our political life. The mere statement of the case is sufficient to show that the incorporation of the American tropics in our national system would essentially transform the constituency of our government, and be fraught with incalculable dangers to the vitality of our democratic institutions. . . .

. . . . .

The annexation of the Hawaiian Islands would be liable to objections of a similar nature. Their population, according to the census of 1890, consists of 34,436 natives, 6,186 half-castes, 7,495 born in Hawaii of foreign parents, 15,301 Chinese, 12,360 Japanese, 8,602 Portuguese, 1,928 Americans, 1,344 British, 1,034 Germans, 227 Norwegians, 70

French, 588 Polynesians, and 419 other foreigners. If there ever was a population unfit to constitute a State of the American Union, it is this. But it is the characteristic population of the islands in that region—a number of semicivilized natives crowded upon by a lot of adventurers flocked together from all parts of the globe to seek their fortunes, some to stay, many to leave again after having accomplished their purpose, among them Chinese and Japanese making up nearly one-fourth of the aggregate. The climate and the products of the soil are those of the tropics, the system of labor corresponding. If attached to the United States, Hawaii would always retain a colonial character. It would be bound to this republic not by a community of interest or national sentiment but simply by the protection against foreign aggression given to it and by certain commercial advantages. No candid American would ever think of making a State of this Union out of such a group of islands with such a population as it has and is likely to have. It would always be to this republic a mere dependency, an outlying domain, to be governed as such. The constitutional question involved in an acquisition of this nature has recently been so conclusively discussed by an eminent jurist, Judge Cooley, that not another word need be said about it. [Thomas M. Cooley, "Grave Obstacles to Hawaiian Annexation," *Forum*, Vol. XV (June, 1893), pp. 389–406.]

But there is a practical feature of the case which deserves the gravest consideration. The Hawaiian Islands are distant two thousand miles from our nearest seaport. Their annexation is advocated partly on commercial grounds, partly for the reason that the islands would furnish very desirable locations for naval depots, coaling stations, and similar conveniences, and that Hawaii is the "key" to something vast and important in that region. Thus we find in favor of the scheme a combination of the interest of commercial adventure with the ambition to make this republic a great naval power which is to play an active and commanding part in the international politics of the world. Leaving aside the question whether the occupation of this "key" would not require for its protection the acquisition of further "keys," admitting for argument's sake all that is claimed for this project, might we not still ask ourselves whether the possession of such an outlying domain two thousand miles away would really be an element of strength to us as against other powers?

In our present condition we have over all the great nations of the world one advantage of incalculable value. We are the only one that is not in any of its parts threatened by powerful neighbors; the only one not under any necessity of keeping up a large armament either on land or water for the security of its possessions; the only one that can turn all the energies of its population to productive employment; the only one that has an entirely free hand. This is a blessing for which the American people can never be too thankful. It should not be lightly jeoparded. . . .

The inestimable advantage of commanding among the nations of the world the greatest degree of consideration and deference without any necessity on our part of keeping up burdensome military and naval establishments we enjoy now and shall continue to enjoy so long as we are so situated that in case of war we can defend all our possessions without leaving our own continental ground, on which we can fight with every condition in our favor.

This advantage will be very essentially impaired if we present to a possible enemy a vulnerable point of attack which we have to defend, but cannot defend without going out of our impregnable stronghold, away from the seat of our power, to fight on ground on which the enemy may appear in superior strength, and have the conditions in *his* favor. Such a vulnerable point will be presented by the Hawaiian Islands if we annex them, as well as by any outlying possession of importance. It will not be denied that in case of war with a strong naval power the defence of Hawaii would require very strong military and naval establishments there, and a fighting fleet as large and efficient as that of the enemy; and in case of a war with a combination of great naval powers, it might require a fleet much larger than that of any of them. Attempts of the enemy to gain an important advantage by a sudden stroke, which would be entirely harmless if made on our continental stronghold, might have an excellent chance of success if made on our distant insular possession, and then the whole war could be made to turn upon that point, where the enemy might concentrate his forces as easily as we, or even more easily, and be our superior on the decisive field of operations. It is evident that thus the immense advantage we now enjoy of a substantially unassailable defensive position would be lost. We would no longer possess the inestimable privilege of being stronger and more secure than any other nation without a large and costly armament. Hawaii, or whatever other outlying domain, would be our Achilles' heel. Other nations would observe it, and regard us no longer as invulnerable. If we acquire Hawaii, we acquire not an addition to our strength, but a dangerous element of weakness.

It is said that we need a large navy in any case for the protection of our commerce, and that if we have it for this purpose it may at the same time serve for the protection of outlying national domains without much extra expense. The premise is false. We need no large navy for the protection of our commerce. Since the extinction of the Barbary pirates and of the Western buccaneers, the sea is the safest public highway in the world. . . . Our commerce is not threatened by anybody or anything, unless it be the competition of other nations and the errors of our own commercial policy; and against these influences war-ships avail nothing. Nor do we need any war-ships to obtain favorable commercial arrangements with other nations. Our position of power under existing circumstances is such that no foreign nation will, at the risk of a quarrel with us, deny our commerce any accommodation we can reasonably lay claim to. . . .

In another respect a large navy might prove to the American people a most undesirable luxury. It would be a dangerous plaything. Its possession might excite an impatient desire to use it, and lead us into strong temptations to precipitate a conflict of arms in case of any difference with a foreign government, which otherwise might easily be settled by amicable adjustment. The little new navy we have has already perceptibly stimulated such a spirit among some of our navy officers and civilian navy enthusiasts, who are spoiling for an opportunity to try the new guns. . . . Every new war-ship we build will be apt further to encourage this tendency; and nothing will be wanting but the growth of the belief among navy officers that they can make themselves heroes of a new era by using their opportunities for carrying on some vigorous foreign policy on their own motion to render the navy the more dangerous to the peace and dignity of this republic the more ships we have. No great power can do so much among the nations of the world for the cause of international peace by the moral forces of its example as the United States. The United States will better fulfill their mission and and more exalt their position in the family of nations by indoctrinating their navy officers in the teachings of Washington's farewell address than by flaunting in the face of the world the destructive power of arms and artillery.

Nothing could be more foolish than the notion we hear frequently expressed that so big a country should have a big navy. Instead of taking pride in the possession of a big navy, the American people ought to be proud of not needing one. This is their distinguishing privilege, and it is their true glory.

The advocates of the annexation policy advance some arguments which require but a passing notice. They say that unless we take a certain country offered to us — Hawaii, for instance — some other power will take it, and that, having refused ourselves, we cannot object. This is absurd. Having shown ourselves unselfish, we shall have all the greater moral authority in objecting to an arrangement which would be obnoxious to our interests.

We are told that unless we take charge of a certain country

it will be ill-governed and get into internal trouble. This is certainly no inducement. This republic cannot take charge of all countries that are badly governed. On the contrary, a country apt to get into internal trouble would be no desirable addition to our national household.

We are told that the people of a certain country wish to join us, and it would be wrong to repel them. But the question whether a stranger is to be admitted as a member of our family is our right and our duty to decide according to our own view of the family interest.

We are told that we need coaling stations in different parts of the world for our navy . . . and that the rich resources of the countries within our reach should be open to American capital and enterprise. There is little doubt that we can secure by amicable negotiation sites for coaling stations which will serve us as well as if we possessed the countries in which they are situated. In the same manner we can obtain from and within them all sorts of commercial advantages. We can own plantations and business houses in the Hawaiian Islands . . . and all this without taking [them] . . . into our national household on an equal footing with the States of our Union, without exposing our political institutions to the deteriorating influence of their participation in our government, without assuming any responsibilities for them which would oblige us to forego the inestimable privilege of being secure in our possessions without large and burdensome armaments. . . .

The fate of the American people is in their own wisdom and will. If they devote their energies to the development of what they possess within their present limits . . . their "manifest destiny" will be the preservation of the exceptional and invaluable advantages they now enjoy, and the growth on a congenial soil of a vigorous nationality in freedom, prosperity, and power. If they yield to the allurement of the tropics and embark in a career of indiscriminate aggrandizement, their "manifest destiny" points with equal certainty to a total abandonment of their conservative traditions of policy, to a rapid deterioration in the character of the people and their political institutions, and to a future of turbulence, demoralization, and final decay.

The Philippines and
the Debate at Flood Tide

*John Barrett and David J. Hill versus
Henry Van Dyke and Frank Parsons*

The debate over American purchase and retention of
the Philippine Islands, following the Spanish-American
War, capsulated and climaxed the dispute of a decade
over insular expansionism. All of the earlier arguments
of both sides appeared to find fresh vindication and
heightened proof. Certainly in the eyes of the
Anti-Imperialists the Philippines Question represented
the very core of the debate and the cause. There could
be no talk now of plots by Prince Bismarck, the rights
of American-born sugar planters, or geographic con-
tiguity. Acquisition of the Philippines would represent
colonialism, naked and shameless. The bolder of the
Imperialists embraced the Philippines Question with
equal confidence. Its acquisition would dramatically en-
hance the diplomatic influence of the United States in
the Far East and witness to the world that America was
prepared to adopt the Large Policy required by the
laws of national growth and the duties demanded of the

great. The articles that follow — by John Barrett and David Hill, spokesmen for the Annexationists, and by Henry Van Dyke and Frank Parsons, champions of self-determination for the Filipino — do not pretend to cover the entire range of arguments offered by either side. They do perhaps suggest the most pronounced points of division — division of policy and temperament and political philosophy.

John Barrett (1866–1938) was a diplomat who tended to adopt the region where he resided, proclaiming its unequaled beauty and strategic value. Appointed by Grover Cleveland as U.S. minister to Siam when only 27, Barrett took the opportunity of a quiet post to travel about the Orient and to send to the periodical press back home a small sheaf of articles extolling Siam and calling upon his fellow Americans to take a larger interest in the Far East. When the Spanish-American War broke out — in support of his predictions and hopes — Barrett resigned his post in Bangkok and hurried to Manila as a war correspondent. Appointing himself an adviser to Commodore George Dewey, Barrett sent to the press and to Washington a stream of news and advice. History was about to see the beginning of the Pacific Era; a nation that would control its destiny must seek to become a Pacific power. Dewey's victory had granted America opportunities equal to its destiny; let America seize these opportunities and pursue a "strong policy" in the Far East. (Several years later Barrett would be appointed a delegate to the Second International Conference of American States in Mexico City. His subsequent career as a diplomat and publicist would center about the Pan American Union and demonstrate his convictions respecting the vital importance of Latin America for the commerce and diplomacy of the United States.)

David Jayne Hill (1850–1932) was more temperate in his imperialism, as befitted one who had been a college president at Bucknell University and the University of Rochester. In 1898 he was Assistant Secretary of State, a post he would hold for five years. Though his influence on the policies of McKinley and Roosevelt was limited, he was valued by those temperamentally diverse Presidents and recognized as a rather special combination of the scholar and the pragmatist. Hill indeed possessed the essential requirements of a No. 2 man: he was not bored by details and was highly skilled at articulating the ideas of others. Not an Expansionist when he came to Washington, Hill made a careful study of the options available to the McKinley Administration after the Spanish-American War and became a moderate Imperialist as the result of conviction as well as loyalty. In his article on "The War and the Extension of Civilization," Hill offered for the Expansionists the most rational and least ethnocentric exposition of the New Mission.

In direct opposition to the arguments of Barrett and Hill are those of the Rev. Henry Van Dyke and Frank Parsons. What all four men shared, however, was an unalloyed sincerity and certitude.

Henry Van Dyke (1852–1933) was a poet, preacher, essayist, professor, and organizer. A devout Presbyterian, he believed that a minister should offer social as well as spiritual instruction; the Brick Presbyterian Church in New York City became under his leadership a center of civic consciousness. To the seven cardinal sins, Van Dyke would add those of political corruption, civic apathy, spoilsmanship, and — with 1898 — imperialism. Where many ministers saw in the acquisition of the Philippine Islands a chance to advance the missionary labors of their denominations, Van Dyke saw it as a moral evil. Tending to identify the truths of the Founding Fathers with those of the Apostles, he saw imperialism as false to Christ as well as America. Not an advocate of isolationism — in 1919 he would be an ardent supporter of the League of Nations — he was a strong opponent of jingoism and what he considered the Bismarckian diplomacy of greed and grab. He stands in the dispute over insular expansionism in the late 1890's as a representative of the strong moralistic flavor that characterized the Anti-Imperialists and their arguments.

A more secularized version of that moralism is offered in the short and angry essay by Frank Parsons (1854–1908). At varying points in his career a railroad engineer, lawyer, and teacher, Parsons found his true forte as an early analyst of pressure-group politics. At varying times a Prohibitionist, a Populist, and a non-Marxian Socialist, he was an advocate of a managed currency, municipal ownership of public utilities, direct legislation, and the self-determination of all nations. Possessed of a passion for justice and a deep-seated suspicion of the political influence of great accumulations of wealth, he feared plutocracy for its corrupting impact on America's diplomacy as well as on her domestic institutions. His particular contribution to the Anti-Imperialist cause was to emphasize the alleged association of finance capitalism and imperialism. More clearly than William Jennings Bryan — whom he supported in the election of 1900 — Parsons sought to link the evils of monopoly, militarism, and expansion.

7. The Problem of the Philippines*

JOHN BARRETT

In the capture and occupation of the Philippines the United States will be confronted by one of the gravest and yet most interesting problems in the history of our foreign relations. The President, Congress — and the people who develop the sentiment that guides the executive and legislative branches of our Government in their acts — have before them, in the determination of what shall be done with the Philippines, a question second only in importance to that of the fate of Cuba, and possibly involving equally serious issues and international complications.

The great European powers and Japan are deeply concerned in the future of the Philippines. They recognize that the nation holding them — if one of the first magnitude — will have a vantage ground of inestimable strategical and commercial value; and they will watch with a more jealous atti-

Originally published in the *North American Review*, Vol. CLXVII (September 1898), pp. 259–67.

* This article — which reached the *Review* only in time for publication now — is unique in its interest because of the fact that it was written before the outbreak of hostilities between Spain and the United States. It addresses itself, nevertheless, to the situation in Eastern waters which has actually resulted from the war, the author having anticipated the question which the brilliant victory of Admiral Dewey suddenly thrust upon public consideration. As is well known, Mr. Barrett has made, for many years, a special study of the countries of the Far East in their relations to the development of American commerce. — Editor, *N.A.R.*

tude the disposition of these islands, matchless in wealth and location, than they will the fate of Cuba.

The Philippines are the southern key to the Far East; they hold a position in the South not much less important than that of Japan in the North; the South China Sea, the pathway of the numberless steamers and ships that come to the Far East by the Suez and Cape Town routes, is under the eye of Manila. . . .

If anyone doubts the strategical and commercial importance of the Philippines, he should obtain a map of the Far East and study carefully that splendid coast line of Eastern Asia that reaches from Singapore and Bangkok to Tientsin and Vladivostock, with its many ports, its mighty rivers, its general greatness and its sheltered seas guarded by such island lands or groups as Japan, Formosa, the Philippines, Borneo, Java and Sumatra. It has no equal in the wide world. And along this coast and among all these islands none stands out more prominently than the Philippines, over which the American flag may yet float. There are those who will call me a dreamer, an enthusiast, and a framer of fantasies, but my conclusions are based on accurate information of the Philippines, their cities, their open ports and their distant inland country. I have . . . myself carefully investigated their resources—forest, agricultural, mineral and animal. . . .

The main point of my argument . . . is that the United States Government, if it seizes the Philippines, should consider deliberately and thoroughly all phases of the question: What shall be the ultimate disposition of the islands in the light of their great strategical and commercial importance?

These four propositions can be outlined as representing the different policies that can be followed by the United States in determining the future of the Philippines:

1. They can be held as a permanent possession, colony, territory, or State of the United States.

2. They can be returned to Spain on the payment of a war indemnity.

3. They can be given their independence.

4. They can be sold to some nation . . . or exchanged for certain of its possessions or for reciprocal advantages.

Of these eventualities it would now seem that the first or fourth is more likely of realization than the second or third. It is a grave question whether Spain would be able to pay such war indemnity as the United States would demand, if a conflict is prolonged and its cost runs into the hundreds of millions. . . . The independence of the islands may sound well, but the reasons for it are far outweighed by those against it. A cardinal point is that the natives themselves are not equal to it. The masses of population are totally unprepared for such a change, and the leaders who are both able and honest are so very few that, were independence granted, the islands would descend into constant civil wars and develop conditions that would either compel the United States to exercise a costly supervision over them, or cause another power, like England, France, Japan or Germany, to take them for the protection of their own interests there. What is more, the natives, including the insurgent leaders, do not themselves expect nor ask for independence. If they are sincere in what they have said to me, and to others who have mingled with them, the chief desideratum they seek is actual and lasting reform of the present abuses, especially the grinding taxation that keeps the majority of them in comparative poverty. Had Spain executed the reforms promised time and time again, or had she deliberately undertaken a system of colonial government such as exists in the British possessions of India or in those of Holland in Java, it is altogether probable that there would be no insurgent party of strength in the Philippines. . . . Were the United States to signify the intention of holding the Philippines as a colony, the natives would be content and drop all agitation for independence and for reforms, knowing that the latter would surely come with the organization of a provisional government.

The proposition to make the Philippines a permanent

possession of the United States will no doubt seem at first impracticable and be strongly opposed as against precedent, traditional policy, and the best interests of the American people. It will be argued that we could never grant actual citizenship to 7,000,000 Philippinos, and that, unless the islands are made a State or an integral part of the Union, we would have no adequate system of government for them, and that the experience would be a sad one. The contention would also be advanced that the expense of fortifying and garrisoning Manila and other points, and of protecting them with an ample naval force, would be a burden we should not undertake to carry. Perhaps the strongest adverse argument will be that the permanent occupation will place us on the same basis with European nations as a foreign colonial power, and make us a party to all international entanglements in either Asia or Europe. . . .

On the other hand, there are grave reasons why we should not surrender this group of islands — more resourceful and greater in area, population and opportunities than Cuba, and so situated as to command the commerce and trade of the Far East and the routes thereof — without careful consideration of the advantages that might follow ownership. . . .

If conditions, precedents, law, the Constitution, and traditional policy are against colonization, is it not possible, after a great war that has no respect for precedents and traditions and evolves entirely new conditions, that our Constitution or laws shall be so modified as to permit a system of colonial or dependent government? If the American people will undertake a mighty war with all its dangers, horrors, and cost, can they be too conservative to permit the passage of such enactments as will provide a safe government for the Philippines, without granting that degree of citizenship in such a colony as will permit actual voting powers in the United States? Other nations, particularly Great Britain, have so perfectly developed this system that we have abundant data and precedent in determining what is the best method.

But what have we to gain by taking possession of the Philippines and holding them as a colony or dependent State?

1. We would have an unsurpassed point in the Far East from which to extend our commerce and trade and gain our share in the immense distribution of material prizes that must follow the opening of China, operating from Manila as a base, as does England from Hong Kong.

2. As England has Hong Kong and Singapore, France Saigon, Germany Kiaochow, Russia Port Arthur, the United States would have the great city of Manila as an American capital in the Far East, from which to extend both our material and moral influence where vast interests are at stake, and through which the United States could keep in closest touch with all developments.

3. We would have, in the Philippines themselves, one of the greatest undeveloped opportunities in all the world — a group of islands with numberless riches and resources awaiting exploitation, and capable of providing a market for a large quantity of our manufactured products.

4. We would have in Manila a large and wealthy city and commercial *entrepôt*, located on one of the finest harbors in the world, and backed up by a country that outranks Japan in variety of resources, but which is not much more developed in the interior than Borneo.

5. The steamers and ships that now ply between San Francisco, Portland, Tacoma and Seattle in the United States, and Yokohama, Shanghai and Hong Kong in the Far East, would either make Manila their ultimate destination or have adequate connections with it, thus placing the ports, merchants, and manufacturers in closer relations with all Asia than ever before.

6. The Islands would easily be self-supporting in the matter of government after they were once placed in running order, and they should provide an abundant revenue for improvements of all kinds, even to harbor defences and other fortifications, thus removing the great danger of proving a

financial burden to ourselves. This is apart from the profits resulting to America and American interests in trade exchange, and in exploiting the resources of this wonderful group. . . .

7. The present situation demonstrates the vital necessity of having a naval (as well as commercial) base in Asiatic waters. The moment neutrality is declared our fleet has no place in which to rendezvous, to coal, or to repair, and is 7,000 miles from the nearest home port! We hope, and are confident, that our ships will be more than a match for the Spanish fleet at Manila, but supposing they are unsuccessful, where can they go to recoup and recoal? . . .

8. The growing importance of the Pacific, of Pacific commerce, Pacific politics, Pacific lands, and the responsibilities resting on the United States in connection with that growth, together with the impending opening of China and the wide reaching effect thereof upon the United States as well as upon Europe, demand that we do not shirk the duty of governing the Philippines, which must play a leading part in all this development. What with the cutting of the Nicaragua Canal, the annexation of Hawaii, the laying of a Pacific cable, the rapid progress of our Pacific Coast interests, the increase in our trade with the Far East, and the necessity of finding wider foreign markets for our surplus products, is it too much to expect that we shall endeavor to hold the Philippines as a permanent possession if we succeed in taking them from Spain?

The other alternative and fourth proposition of ultimate disposal — that of selling to another power or exchanging for reciprocal advantages — is assuredly worthy of practical investigation, but there are two very serious obstacles in the way. One is that few if any powers would pay our price, or give us in exchange what we would ask. Another is the probable objection of other European powers to one of their number obtaining such an overwhelming advantage in the East as would plainly result from the possession of the Philippines, and the vigorous protests that would be aroused, which in time might lead to most serious diplomatic differences with countries whose good will we would otherwise keep. . . .

In conclusion, it behooves me to state that these opinions and arguments are written before war is declared between Spain and the United States, but when the announcement is momentarily expected. . . . Whether we capture and hold the Philippines, or Spain shall successfully resist our efforts, on the one hand, or war shall not bring us face to face with the specific problems outlined, the truth remains, beyond question or quibble, that now is the critical time when the United States should strain every nerve and bend all her energies to keep well to the front in the mighty struggle that has begun for the supremacy of the Pacific Seas. If we seize the opportunity we may become leaders forever, but if we are laggards now we will remain laggards until the crack of doom. The rule of the survival of the fittest applies to nations as well as to the animal kingdom. It is a cruel, relentless principle being exercised in a cruel, relentless competition of mighty forces; and these will trample over us without sympathy or remorse unless we are trained to endure and strong enough to stand the pace.

8. The War and the Extension of Civilization
DAVID J. HILL

The year just closed has revealed more than any other in a century of extraordinary development the extent of the energies inherent in the American people. The idea of disinterested duty, which has seldom animated nations, has nerved the Republic to the prosecution of a costly foreign war, as the result of which a decadent system of colonial

Originally published in the *Forum*, Vol. XXVII (February 1899), pp. 650–55 .

exploitation has been swept out of existence, and our flag is found floating in triumph on distant seas.

If the war with Spain was a necessity imposed by "humanity" and "civilization," these principles do not cease to be imperative in the moment of victory. Whatever justified the war has demanded a peace in harmony with its motives; and it was, therefore, the desire and the duty of the Chief Executive of the nation to secure by treaty, through his commissioners, the great ends for which the war was undertaken.

Expressed in a single phrase, the purpose of the American people in assuming the task of intervention was "enforced pacification." A strife rendered interminable by resistance to oppression, on the one hand, and by administrative incapacity, on the other, demanded the interference of a Power strong enough to command a cessation of hostilities. If the theatre of our intervention was unexpectedly extended by our victories in the Pacific, the principles upon which it was based were not thereby modified; and a duty clearly recognized in the case of Cuba became equally imperative in the Philippines.

When the Peace Commissioners of the United States met those of Spain at Paris, it had become evident to our Government that there was no logical justification of the war which did not involve the abdication of Spanish sovereignty in all the territories in question. To claim the abdication of Spanish rule over Cuba and Puerto Rico and to permit it to continue over the Philippines, would have been to assert that our motives and purposes were different from those which really inspired and authorized our war for Cuba.

It was, therefore, a moral and logical necessity that Spain should surrender her islands in the Pacific as well as those in the Atlantic. And, if we consider the history of the Philippines, it is still more clearly evident that their loss to Spain was a fitting conclusion of the recent war. Conquered originally by a fleet sent out from Mexico in 1564, they were a natural adjunct of her American possessions. . . .

By another course of development, the feeble colonies
planted on the Atlantic coast of North America have spread
their civilization to the Pacific, and their institutions over the
whole continent. Hawaii, colonized and developed by American enterprise, has become a part of our national territory.
California . . . carries on a great Pacific trade by steam. A
submarine cable will soon connect our western shores with
Asia; and an interoceanic canal, wedding the Atlantic and the
Pacific, will not only shorten the sailing-distance between our
coasts by 10,000 miles, but will bring Boston nearer than
Liverpool to Polynesia, Japan, and Northern China.

To the eyes of foreign observers, the opportunities for
empire presented to the American Republic by existing conditions seem enviable, and may even excite the suspicion of
being intentionally sought. The organization of
"anti-imperialistic" societies among us, — a proceeding which
implies a belief that some other portion of the American
people seriously desires to extend an imperial sway over
distant regions, — tends to confirm this false conception in the
minds of foreigners, and does a great wrong to the motives
and principles of this nation; for the thirst for foreign domination, and the passion for self-enrichment by the plunder of
defenceless races, which have created the great empires of
the past, are repugnant to our Constitution as well as to our
people, none of whom have taken the pains to organize an
imperial policy.

There are two propositions upon which, it would seem, all
true Americans can solidly unite: (1) That we shall not suffer
the peoples in whose behalf we have intervened to relapse
into anarchy; and (2) that we shall not permit the exploitation
of defenceless populations under our protection by the methods of the very system which we have just destroyed. To
repudiate these propositions, is to repudiate the ethical and
logical justification of the war.

The more closely we subject the matter to analysis, the
more clearly we perceive that we have been waging a war not

of conquest, but of civilization. There are two ways of neu-
tralizing its normal results and of repudiating its animating
principles. One of these is to employ the methods which we
have succeeded in destroying; the other is to drop the whole
enterprise in its state of incompletion and to confess our error
in having undertaken it. Equally with the so-called "imperialists"—if any really exist—the "anti-imperialists" offend
against the principle upon which the United States has thus
far acted. That principle has been expressed as the right and
duty of our Government "in the name of humanity, in the
name of civilization," to enforce the end of strife and to
secure a rule of justice. To abandon in a critical moment the
populations emancipated from the sovereignty of Spain, may
seem more respectable than to exploit them; but neither the
one nor the other is in harmony with the conception of national duty which inspired the prosecution of the war. There
are only three possible positions to be taken upon the question of our proper relations to the late colonies of Spain: (1)
That Spain had a right to exploit them, and, since we have
defeated her, that we have succeeded to that right; (2) that
Spain was wrong in her treatment of her colonies, but that we
had no right to interfere; and (3) that Spain was wrong to an
extent that justified our interference and our substitution of a
better order. Those who accept the last position must admit
that our duty has not been fully performed until we have
substituted a better order than we found,—in truth, the best
order we are able to secure.

Having invoked "humanity" and "civilization" as the
watchwords of the war, they now clearly prescribe our task in
imposing peace. The current course of events has been described by its enemies as "imperialism," and by its friends as
"expansion"; but neither of these terms quite accurately
meets the case. The purpose of our Government has not been
the subjection of foreign peoples for the sake of empire, nor
the enlargement of our territorial limits for the sake of expansion. Both of these words imperfectly express the sit-

uation, and, thus far at least, are not true to history. A more fitting term to designate the aims and achievements of the nation is, perhaps, the phrase "the extension of civilization"; for it expresses the motive and controlling principle of the war and of the treaty by which, when ratified, it is to be concluded.

The real problem of the moment is, How can the permanent peace, for which the war was fought, be best secured? By the terms of the Treaty of Paris, the sovereign power of the United States has a clear field for the exercise of its peaceful intentions. Nothing short of this unqualified opportunity could have satisfied the just expectations of the American people; and this fact alone is the sufficient justification of the work thus far accomplished. In the midst of the questions which now agitate the public mind there is one clear certainty; namely, that the presence of the Stars and Stripes is the best security against international intrigue, chronic revolution, and every form of violence to the inalienable rights of man. . . .

It is sometimes alleged that, because we are a self-governing people, we are disqualified for governing others. Every step of our national progress has excited the fears of men who have believed that republican institutions could be safe only in some secluded community lying within narrow boundaries. . . . Every step of territorial extension has been followed by a spasm of hysterics over the possible dissolution of the Republic; but each in turn has vindicated the wisdom of confidence in man and the power of great principles. The annexation of Louisiana, which doubled the area of the country at one stroke, developed our inland navigation; and the addition of California stimulated the construction of our great railway system. New inventions, enlarged enterprises, increased prosperity, and a stronger sense of national unity have followed every territorial extension, and augmented the influence of the Republic among the nations. And now that isolation is no longer possible, with a growing foreign trade that already extends over the globe, shall we doubt that new outposts of defence and influence, unified by a waterway uniting the eastern ocean with the western, — at the same time reducing, by more than half, the sailing-distance between our Atlantic and Pacific coasts, and thereby doubling the efficiency of our navy, — would create new markets for our merchandise, and place the seal of security upon the designs of peace?

It would, indeed, be an anomaly if the best form of government on earth, as we believe ours to be, were incapable of extension by virtue of its excellence. It is true that it is not in its fulness adapted to nations still in their minority. . . . Our territorial administration has always recognized a period of tutelage as a normal political condition; and millions of men have been happy and prosperous under it. Our Constitution was framed and has always been applied with a distinct consciousness that, while men are equal in natural rights, such as life, liberty, and the pursuit of happiness, political rights are the creations of law, not the gifts of nature. No theory of republicanism has ever maintained that maturity in statecraft, or even any degree of political capacity, is essential to every unit of the population. As distinctly as a monarchy a republic must make provision for its natural wards. . . .

. . . . .

At the present moment this nation holds in trust the liberties of nearly twelve millions of human beings. When at last it renders an account of its stewardship, what will its answer be? Shall it say to the Lord of Nations, "Here is that which is thine; I have hid it in a napkin, and buried it in the earth; behold thy treasure undiminished"? Or shall it say, "With thy talent I have gathered increase. Behold the wilderness now populous with thriving cities; behold the sea made the highway of human intercourse; behold its islands, no longer bleeding under the sword, but blossoming with plenty, and smiling in the security of peace"? The true glory of a nation is not in

the spoils of conquest, but in the fruits of the faithful hus-
bandman; and what a glorious harvest is the ripening of a
civic consciousness matured under liberty secured by law!

9. The American Birthright and the Philippine Pottage

HENRY VAN DYKE

*A Thanksgiving sermon preached in the Brick Presbyterian
Church, New York City, November 24, 1898.*

This is the most important Thanksgiving Day that has been
celebrated by the present generation of Americans. . . . This
Thanksgiving Day is not significant alone in its causes for
gratitude. It is an important day, a marked day, an immensely
serious day because it finds us, suddenly and without preparation, face to face with the most momentous and perilous
problem of our national history.

The question that came upon us at the close of the Revolution was serious: Should the liberated colonies separate, or
should they unite? But the leaders of the people had been
long preparing to meet it; and the irresistible pressure of
reason and sympathy consolidated the nation.

The question that came upon us in the Civil War was
urgent and weighty: Could the Republic continue to exist
"half slave, half free?" But again the minds of the wise and
fearless were ready with the well-considered answer, wrought
out after painful years of conflict. Slavery must die that the
Republic might live.

The question that comes upon us to-day is vaster, more
pressing, more fraught with incalculable consequences.
Silently and swiftly it flashes out of a clear sky.

Originally published in *The Independent,* Vol. L (December 1, 1898), pp.
1579–85.

Are the United States to continue as a peaceful Republic, or are they to become a conquering empire? Is the result of the war with Spain to be the banishment of European tyranny from the Western Hemisphere, or is it to be the entanglement of the Western Republic in the rivalries of European Kingdoms? Have we set the Cubans free, or have we lost our own faith in freedom? Are we still loyal to the principles of our forefathers, or are we now ready to sell the American birthright for a mess of pottage in the Philippines? Nine months ago no one dreamed of such a question. Not one American in five hundred could have told you what or where the Philippines were: if any one thought of their possession as a possible result of the war, he kept the thought carefully concealed.

Six months ago, while Admiral Dewey's triumphant fleet was resting in Cavite Bay, there were not fifty people in the country who regarded his victory as the first step in a career of imperial conquest in the Far East: the question of reversing a whole national policy and extending our dominion at one stroke of the sword over a vast and populous group of islands in the China Sea was utterly unconsidered.

Without warning, without deliberation, and apparently without clear intention, it has been made the burning question of the day. Never has fate sprung a more trying surprise upon an unsuspecting and ingenuous people; never has the most momentous problem of a great republic been met so hastily, so lightly, or with such inconsiderate confidence; and, as if to add to the irony of the situation, political leaders assure us not only that the question has been raised unintentionally, but also that it has been already settled involuntarily. Without any adequate discussion, without any popular vote, without any intelligent and responsible leadership, by a mysterious and non-resident destiny, by the accident that a Spanish fleet destroyed on the first of May, 1898 was in the harbor of Manila instead of on the high seas, the future career of the American Republic has been changed irrevocably; the nation has been committed to a policy of colonial expansion; and the United States of America have been transformed into the "United States and Conquered Territories of America and the China Sea." Surely this is the veriest comedy of self-government, the most ridiculous blind man's buff of national development that ever a scorner of democracy dared to imagine. If it were true, it would be a most humorous commentary on the Declaration of Independence and a farcical finale of the American Revolution.

But, fortunately, it is not true. There is an old-fashioned document called the American Constitution which was expressly constructed to discourage the unconscious humor of such sudden changes. Before the die is cast the people must be taken fairly into the game; before the result is irrevocable, the Supreme Court must pass upon the rules and the play. The question whether the American birthright is to be bartered for the Philippine pottage is still open. A brief, preliminary discussion of this question will not be out of place this morning.

I wish to confine the question to the form in which it is put. The case of Cuba does not enter into it. There is no proposal at present to do anything more for Cuba than we promised: to guarantee peace, order and free government to a neighboring people. That is a fine thing to do. Nor do the cases of the Hawaiian Islands and Puerto Rico enter clearly into the question. The legal government of Hawaii has asked for annexation to the United States; Puerto Rico is a small island, close at hand, and inhabited principally by white people who have received us willingly and are already asking for territorial government. Whatever danger there may be in taking such territories under our flag, there is at least no flagrant violation of American principles.

But in the case of the Philippines there is a glaring difference. No man of intelligence ventures to deny it; many openly rejoice in the difference. The proposal to annex, by force, or purchase, or forcible purchase, these distant, unwilling and semi-barbarous islands is hailed as a new and glorious departure in American history. It is frankly confessed that it involves a departure from ancient traditions; it is openly boasted that it leaves the counsels of Washington and Jefferson far behind us forever. Because of this novelty, because of this separation from what we once counted a most precious heritage, I venture to ask whether this bargain offers any fit compensation for the loss of our American birthright.

Let us consider the arguments in favor of it. They may be summed up under three heads: the argument from Duty, the argument from Destiny and the argument from Desperation.

1. The argument from Duty comes first because it is the strongest. Undoubtedly we have incurred responsibilities by the late war, and we must meet them in a manly spirit. But certainly these responsibilities are not unlimited. They are bounded on one side by our rights. The very question at issue is whether we have a right to deny the principles of our Constitution by conquering unwilling subjects and annexing tributary colonies to our domain. On the other side, our responsibilities are bounded by our abilities. It is never a duty to attempt a task for which one is not fitted. We surely owe the Filipinos the very best that we can give them consistently with our other responsibilities. But it is far from being certain that the best thing we can do for them is to make them our vassals. If that were true our whole duty would not be done, the humane results of the war would not be completed, until we had annexed the misgoverned Spaniards of Spain also. No argument drawn from our duty to an oppressed and suffering race can be applied to the conquest of the Philippine Islands which does not apply with equal and even with greater force to the conquest of the Iberian Peninsula.

2. The argument from Destiny is not an argument; it is a phrase. It takes for granted all that is in dispute. It clothes itself in glittering rainbows and introduces the question of debate in the disguise of a fact accomplished. "Yesterday," says a brilliant orator, "there were four great nations ruling

the world and dividing up the territories of barbarous tribes, — Great Britain, Russia, France and Germany. To-day there are five, for America has entered the arena of colonial conquest." But how came the great Republic in that strange copartnership? By what device was she led blindfold into that curious company? What does she there? What must she forfeit to obtain her share in the partition of spoils? That is the question. To talk of destiny is not to discuss, but to dodge the point at issue.

3. The argument from Desperation directly contradicts the argument from Destiny. It presents the annexation of the Philippines, not as a glorious accomplishment, but as a hard necessity. We must do it because there is nothing else that we can do. A speaker less brilliant than the orator of the Five Nations, but more cautious, puts the case in a sentence: "We have got a wolf by the ears and we can't let go." The answer to this is simple. We have not got the wolf at present, tho we are trying our best to get hold of him. It is absurd to say that the only way for us to get out of our difficulties is to go into the enterprise of wolf-keeping. Granting that the Philippines need a strong hand to set them in order, it has not been shown that ours is the only hand. A protectorate for a limited time and with the purpose of building up a firm self-government would be one of the possible solutions of the difficulty. To pass this by, and say that our only resort is to assume the sovereignty of these as yet unconquered islands, is merely to beg the question.

No, these contradictory arguments from duty and destiny and despair do not touch the real spring of the movement for colonial expansion. It is the prospect of profit that makes those distant islands gleam before our fancy as desirable acquisitions. It is the unconscious desire of rivaling England in her colonial wealth and power that allures us to the untried path of conquest. It is a secret discontent with the part of a peaceful, industrious, self-contained nation that urges us to take an armed hand in the partition of the East and exchange our birthright for a mess of pottage.

Let us weigh the arguments against such a bargain.

1. It is contrary to the Constitution of the United States as interpreted by the Supreme Court. There is no possibility of mistake about the matter. It has been decided by the final authority of that magnificent tribunal in which the Anglo-Saxon ideal of the supremacy of law is forever embodied, more clearly and powerfully than in any other human institution. That court, which is the central glory of our system and the safeguard of our liberties, has said:

There is certainly no power given by the Constitution to the Federal Government to establish or maintain colonies bordering on the United States or at a distance, to be ruled and governed at its own pleasure. . . . No power is given to acquire a territory to be held and governed permanently in that character. — *Supreme Court, Scott vs. Sandford,* December, 1856. . . .

2. Every following step in that new career will bring us into conflict with our own institutions and necessitate constitutional change or insure practical failure. Our Government, with its checks and balances, with its prudent and conservative divisions of power, is the best in the world for peace and self-defense, but the worst in the world for what the President called, a few months ago, "criminal aggression." We cannot compete with monarchies and empires in the game of land-grabbing and vassal ruling. We have not the machinery, and we cannot get it except by breaking up our present system of government and building a new fabric out of the pieces. The supposed analogy between England and America is a fatal illusion. British institutions are founded . . . on the doctrine of inequality. American institutions are founded on the doctrine of equality. If we become a colonizing power we must abandon our institutions or be paralyzed by them. The swiftness of action, the secrecy not to say slipperiness of policy, and the absolutism of control which are essen-

tial to success in territorial conquest and dominion are inconsistent with republicanism as America has interpreted it.
Imperialism and democracy, militarism and self-government,
are contradictory terms. A government of the people, by the
people, for the people is impregnable for defense but impotent
for conquest. When imperialism comes in at the door democracy flies out the window. An imperialistic democracy is
an impossible hybrid. We might as well speak of an atheistic
religion or a white blackness. To enter upon a career of
colonial expansion with our present institutions is to court
failure or to prepare for revolution.

3. There is an equally serious objection to the attempt to
launch the United States upon the business of acquiring vassal colonies and governing distant and inferior races, in the
character of our people and their poor equipment for such a
task.

It is said that we must begin or we shall never learn. The
trouble is that we have already begun, but we have not
learned. . . .

Does the comparison of the treatment of the Indians in
Canada and in the United States give us a comfortable sense
of pride? Is the condition of drunken and disorderly Alaska a
just encouragement to larger colonial enterprises? Is our success in treating the Chinese problem and the Negro problem
so notorious that we must attempt to repeat it on a larger
scale ten thousand miles away? The rifle-shots that ring from
Illinois and the Carolinas, announcing a bloody skirmish of
races in the very heart of the republic, — are these the joyous
salutes that herald our advance to rule eight million more of
black and yellow people in the islands of the Pacific Ocean?
. . . With our unsolved problems staring us in the face, our
cities misgoverned and our territories neglected, the cry of
to-day, — not the cry of despair, but the cry of hope and
courage, — must be "Americans for America!"

4. Another weighty argument against the annexation of the

Philippines is the frightful burden which it will almost certainly impose upon the people.

First, a burden of military service. If we do this thing we dare not do it half-way. A great colonial power must have an army and a navy equal to any in the world. An expansion of territory to a line ten thousand miles away means a new frontier of danger which can only be defended by an enormous armament. No one can tell how large a military force we must ultimately create. But this any one can foretell; the ranks must be kept full; and if Americans do not thirst for garrison duty in the tropics they must be compelled or bought to serve. On the one hand we see a system of conscription like that of Germany, where every man-child is born with a soldier's collar around his neck. On the other hand, we see an enormous drain upon the earnings of the people, like England's annual budget of $203,000,000 for the army and navy.

Second, a burden of heavy taxation. The cost of militarism comes out of the pockets of the people. So far as armies and navies are needed, their expense must be cheerfully borne. I am no advocate of parsimony in national defense. . . . But to wilfully increase our need of military force by an immense and unnecessary extension of our frontier of danger, is to bind a heavy burden and lay it upon the unconscious backs of future generations of toiling men. If we enter the course of foreign conquest, the day is not far distant when we must spend in annual preparation for war more than the $180,000,000 that we now spend every year in the education of our children for peace.

Third, a burden of interminable and bloody strife. Expansion means entanglement. Entanglement means ultimate conflict. The great nations of Europe are encamped around the China Sea in arms. If we go in among them we must fight when they fight. . . .

Colonial expansion means coming strife. The annexation of the Philippines means the annexation of a new danger to the world's peace. The acceptance of imperialism means that we must prepare to beat our plow-shares into swords and our pruning-hooks into spears, and be ready to water distant lands and stain foreign seas with an incalculable and ever-increasing torrent of American blood. Is it for this that philanthropists and Christian preachers urge us to abandon our peaceful mission of enlightenment, our glorious isolation of eminence, and thrust forward, sword in hand, into the arena of imperial conflict.

5. But the chief argument against the forcible extension of American sovereignty over the Philippines is that it certainly involves the surrender of our American birthright. "The imitation of Old World methods," said one of our most powerful journals a few months ago, "by the New World, appears to us to be based upon an entire disregard, not merely of American precedents, but of American principles." (*The Outlook*, July 2, 1898)

I do not speak now of our word of honor, tacitly pledged to the world when we disclaimed "any disposition or intention to exercise any sovereignty, jurisdiction or control over said islands, except for the pacification thereof." It is said that this was a limited promise, that it was meant to be taken in a Pickwickian sense, that it applies only to the island of Cuba. Pass it by.

But how can we pass by the solemn and majestic claim of our Declaration of Independence, that "government derives its just powers from the consent of the governed?" How can we abandon the principle for which our fathers fought and died, "No taxation without representation?" How can we face the world as a union of free States holding vassal States in subjection, a mighty mongrel nation in which a republic is tied to an empire and democracy bears children not to be distinguished from the offspring of absolutism?

Then indeed the glory will have departed from us. Then our emblem of liberty enlightening the world must be changed

to a graven image of power grasping the spoils. Then we shall
mourn our birthright sold for a mess of pottage. . . .

10. Preservation of the Republic:
The Giant Issue of 1900

FRANK PARSONS

The problem of the Trust and the problem of private monopoly in finance are questions of vital moment; but the giant
issue now is whether our flag shall stand for freedom or
oppression. It is vastly important to know whether our governments and industries are to be managed in the interest of a
few or in the interest of all; but it is still more important to
know whether the people approve the policy of abandoning
the Declaration of Independence, turning the Republic into
an Empire, and transforming a peaceful democracy into an
imperial conqueror. The supreme issue is whether the stain of
conquest that blots our flag shall stay upon its folds or be
washed out forever in a flood of patriot votes from the liber-
ty-lovers of the land.

At bottom, all the issues named are one. The same
influence and control that have swept us into foreign aggression are largely responsible for oppression at home.

The Cubans were battling for independence, and the
United States took arms to end the Spanish despotism and
help the Cubans establish a government of their own. The
Filipinos were also in revolt against Spain. They had an army
of 30,000 men. They conquered and captured 10,000 Spanish
soldiers, and, modeling their government on ours, established
law and order and self-government throughout the islands,
with the single exception of the city of Manila. A nation great

Originally published in *The Arena*, Vol. XXIII (June 1900), pp. 561–65.

enough and good enough to help the Cubans throw off the yoke of Spain and establish the independence for which they were fighting should have been great and good enough to have helped the Filipinos also throw off the sixteenth century despotism and establish the independence for which *they* were fighting. Yet the very forces set in motion to free the Cubans have been used by our government as the means of subjugating the Filipinos. Cubans and Filipinos fighting side by side (for physical distance has nothing to do with the essence of the case) against the same despotism, struggling with equal heroism for liberty and independence, and with a success even greater in the Philippines than in Cuba, and our government, *the government of the leading Republic of the world,* steps in to take Cuba from Spanish despotism and establish Cuban independence, and at the same time takes the Philippines from Spanish despotism and establishes an American despotism in its place!

Till the hour we bought the Filipinos at $2.50 per head, like so many cattle passing with the land, and forced the purchase at the point of the bayonet, our flag was the emblem of freedom the wide world over and the hope of the oppressed of every clime; to-day its starry folds are stained with the blood of Filipino patriots fighting against it for their freedom — and to one heroic people it has ceased to be the emblem of liberty and has become the hated symbol of oppression. All the commerce of the East cannot atone for that deep blot. And we could have had all the commerce with the Filipinos free that we have with the same people in subjection. Our commerce can capture all the markets it deserves without a bayonet in its hands.

Admiral Dewey says the Filipinos are as capable of self-government as the Cubans . . . and the fact that they had actually established an admirable system of democratic government clearly proves their capacity. If our government had treated them the same as the Cubans; if the President had announced at the start that the same principles would be applied in the Philippines as in Cuba, and that independence and self-government would be established under an international guarantee of peace and order in the islands, or under such an American protectorate as might be agreeable to the people of the islands and ratified by them, there would have been no war of conquest under the Stars and Stripes. . . .

Is it fair for a nation that owes its own independence to a war fought out upon the clear-cut issue that "governments derive their just powers from the consent of the governed" to establish a government in another country without the consent of the governed?

The Golden Rule lies shattered beneath a policy of aggressive war—torn, like the Declaration of Independence, into useless fragments by our cannon in the Philippines. When we were fighting for independence in 1776, suppose the Filipinos had been strong enough and mean enough to buy us up—get a tax bill to us from the British Empire—and had sent an army over here to subjugate us: where is the difference under the Golden Rule?

We can no longer claim to be a bona-fide, whole-souled Republic. We are an empire—a sort of republic at home and a despotism abroad; a "benevolent" despotism, perhaps (though that remains to be seen), but none the less a despotism. We should not regard a conqueror as anything but a despot if he forced his will upon us, no matter how much he might protest that he was doing it for our benefit. We are civilizing the Filipinos, it is said—shooting it into them and pouring it into them from our saloons, which are more deadly even than our guns. We are not aiming to establish free government in the Philippines. It is not to be a government of the people by the people and for the people. The supreme power is to be lodged in officers appointed by a foreign government, holding its sovereignty by force of arms. It is not expansion, but imperialism. Expansion is the addition of new territory as part of the Republic. This addition does not enlarge the Republic — the *Republic* is no bigger than before. The government merely rules as imperial master over some islands not incorporated in the Republic, but belonging to it as England belonged to the Conqueror, and constituting with it The New American Empire. We have taken the first step that led Rome from the virtues of a self-defending republic to the vices of imperial despotism and the final destruction of liberty at home as well as abroad.

A government that engages in a war of conquest and enslaves a foreign people can no longer stand before the world as a champion of freedom and human rights. Such a government naturally sympathizes with England against the Boers. . . . No matter that the Boers are fighting for freedom against the same oppressor that our fathers struggled with in the dawn of our greatness; no matter that justice and liberty and brotherhood are all on the side of the Boer; no matter that the civilized world is in duty bound to condemn any nation that goes to war in refusal of arbitration — our government cannot be just and manly with England because it is committing the same sort of iniquity in the Philippines. Columbia has turned her face from the dawn and is looking back toward the night that has passed — imperialism abroad and industrial feudalism at home.

Strange things are happening in America when an Administration representing the party of Lincoln — the party that freed the blacks — stands squarely against liberty in the Philippines and sympathizes with a capitalistic war of conquest in South Africa. There is every reason to believe that such an Administration does not truly represent the Republican party. The best sentiment of the "Grand Old Party" is against the present policy of those in power. It is to be hoped that conscience may outweigh partizanship, and men of every party who love liberty and justice may unite to reaffirm the principles of the Declaration of Independence, repair so far as possible the wrong that has been done in the Philippines, and set America right once more on the supreme issue of Democracy or Despotism.

The Panama Canal and
the Debate Continued

Boston Daily Advertiser *versus New York* World

The acquisition of the Panama Canal Zone, though falling outside the chronological limits of the 1890's, is integrally related to the ambitions and debates of that decade.

The general outline of Roosevelt's Canal diplomacy is well known. The points of controversy concerned neither documents nor chronology but questions of interpretation. Did the Panamanian revolutionaries have foreknowledge of Roosevelt's support for their revolution? Did they have foreknowledge of Roosevelt's intention to interpret the old Colombian–U.S. Treaty of 1846 against the interests of Colombia? Did the presence of the U.S.S. *Nashville* inspire the Panamanian revolution or merely protect it? Did Roosevelt connive and conspire to achieve the secession of Panama, or was he the skilled opportunist who was not tardy in accepting the gift of a benevolent Providence?

As these questions are still argued today, so were they debated by such contemporaries as the editors of the Boston *Daily Advertiser* and the New York *World*.

11. Expression of Support

BOSTON DAILY ADVERTISER EDITORIALS

Editorial from the Boston Daily Advertiser, *November 16, 1903*

AN ACT OF NECESSITY

. . . The case was plain. President Roosevelt believed the people of the United States wanted the Panama Canal. Colombia set a higher price than the president was willing to pay. . . . All Europe is glad enough to have the United States build the canal at its own expense. If President Roosevelt wanted to annex all Colombia, not a king, emperor, or president in Europe would say one word to the contrary. The right of the United States in this matter of a canal is by a sort of "eminent domain," not based on international law but on national necessity, as the president looks at it.

It may not be international law. But it is the common practice. Russia wants Finland, or Manchuria. Japan wants Korea. . . . The United States wants Panama. So long as no other nation objects, the big power takes what it wants. If two nations want the same country, there may be trouble. . . .

As things are, the United States technically is not on record as having done anything. The accommodating Sr. Varilla has done all that was necessary. He knew what the United States wanted and he had it done. The Democrats who have been clamoring for the record on the Panama case may search it through. They will find no campaign material for the dealings with Varilla are not included in the documents sent to congress. The United States was pledged to "keep the peace" on the isthmus. . . . And now it will "keep the peace" by preventing any further fighting, as no Colombian forces will be allowed near Panama. . . .

Editorial from the Boston Daily Advertiser, *November 17, 1903*

A USELESS PROTEST

. . . What the Colombian government expects to gain by protesting to any European power against the United States is a puzzle. There is not a power in Europe which is not glad that the United States is doing what President Roosevelt has mapped out to be done. . . . There is a principle (not found in any hand book of international law, but seen everywhere today) in the practice of the civilized powers. It is that no small or backward nation has the right to interfere or to stand in the way of a great national policy determined by a world power. . . .

12. Expression of Dissent

NEW YORK WORLD EDITORIAL

Editorial from the New York World, *November 8, 1903*

THE ROOSEVELT DOCTRINE

The new reading of President Monroe's famous message, which may or may not pass into history as "The Roosevelt Doctrine," seems to be, as revealed by the Panama incident:

1. No great power except the United States shall bully a little South American nation.
2. No European power shall interfere with such bullying when the United States finds it convenient to resort to it.

Mr. Roosevelt's proper instructions to our isthmian representative to recognize a "de facto" government of Panama

"when established," and his wholly improper advice to Colombia to make peace with the "Government of Panama,"
which he assumes to exist, leaves European public opinion
still in that "distant and cynical" temper which *The World*
predicted. . . .

There is even approval of it. The London *Post* says that it
is "in the interests of the world and of civilization" that
Panama should secede under our chaperonage. The "interests
of civilization" are the interests of shop. It is pleasanter for
European merchants upon the isthmus to do business in a
"republic" "protected" by the United States than in the usual
tropical anarchy. Nor does the farce of independence deceive
any one. The London *Mail* speaks of the President's action as
"virtual annexation," and says:

Thus the United States after absorbing Spanish possessions in the
Caribbean will draw a step nearer to the immense wealth of South
America, which must one day fall under its control.

But there are still to be reckoned with, the American Congress and the American people. What will they say of a
palpably "arranged" revolution? Of an immediate recognition
of a rebel state such as for years we forbade Europe to accord
to our Confederacy? Of the President's interference to pre-
vent Colombia from waging war as we did. . . .

As to the canal, our sole and shabby excuse, *The World*
repeats:

We can dig the canal by the Nicaragua route if Colombia refuses to
treat. We can, if need be, do without a canal. We cannot forget or
safely ignore American precedents and ideals which bid us as
scrupulously to avoid secret "understandings" with Central American insurgents as "entangling alliances" with European monarchies.

It is the present duty of Congress to call for the innermost
facts as to this "revolution" plotted on our shores and to
consider what amends can now be made to a nation despoiled
by what is practically armed intervention.

Territorial Expansion and Commercial Gain

Albert J. Beveridge versus George F. Hoar

On January 9, 1900, the newly elected senator from Indiana Albert J. Beveridge brought to a conclusion a long oration in praise of the Philippine Islands, the American soldier, and the March of the Flag. Scorning the need to cloak that march in the gauze of humanitarian obligation, Beveridge boldly trumpeted the economic resources of the Philippines and their potential value for the expansion of our Far Eastern trade. In the midst of the ovation that followed, one senator sought to gain the recognition of the presiding officer. When finally he succeeded, George Frisbie Hoar of Massachusetts tried to chastise his new colleague by references to an older and purer day, when statesmen appealed to right and not profit and when the goal of the Republic was not gain but justice.

It was an interesting encounter, one that symbolized not only the changing mood of a party and the shifting composition of its leadership but also the increasing significance of economic arguments as the debate over

Imperialism reached its climax. Those arguments had been offered with equal clarity, however, in certain letters of both men some months earlier. For the younger man, territorial expansion was necessary to the nation's economic growth and industrial prosperity; for the older man territorial expansion represented the probable destruction of America's special mission and natural commercial expansion.

Albert Beveridge (1862–1927) was the self-conscious personification of Young America, prepared to meet the challenge of a new century and ride the wave of a future that pointed to dominance for the strong and profits for the quick. A graduate of DePauw, Beveridge won his first fame as a boy orator and rose swiftly in the ranks of the state Republican Party in Indiana. Later to win fame for his interest in domestic issues and his identification with the Progressive Movement, Beveridge in the 1890's associated his political career with the associated goals of trade expansion and diplomatic virility. The nation's diplomacy should seek to insure the absorption of surplus production and the expansion of American markets. The flag and the trader must march in step.

George Frisbie Hoar (1826–1904), senior senator from Massachusetts, found such arguments distasteful as well as erroneous. A man with the face of Mr. Pickwick and the apprehensions of the prophet Jeremiah, Hoar came to politics as a charter Republican and as an antagonist of the Slavocracy. By 1898 he had served in Congress for three decades and saw himself as the spokesman of the true faith of his section and party. Though not without a modest amount of political skill, he was suspicious of those who obeyed the demands of party regularity too readily or enjoyed the game of politics too openly. The true model for a Republican senator was Charles Sumner. As Sumner had exposed the errors of Grant's annexationist scheme for Santo Domingo, so now other faithful Republicans must correct the unfortunate course of the foreign policy of the McKinley Administration. America had grown powerful through diplomatic abstinence, and her commerce had flourished through the peaceful instrumentalities of the Yankee entrepreneur and trader. Gunboat diplomacy was false to the advice of the Founding Fathers and false to the economic health of the nation.

13. "Territorial extension ... an incident of commercial extension"

ALBERT J. BEVERIDGE

Albert J. Beveridge to George W. Perkins, May 3, 1898. Indianapolis.

... With this mail I hand you my recent speech in Boston, which I have marked. I delivered that speech in the very home of Mugwumpery; in a town where it was supposed to be that the blood of its citizens was so cold that it no longer had American enterprise; but when I came to that point where I advocated the extension of our territory, there was a greater demonstration even than there was at the Delmonico dinner. . . .

I have no words sufficiently withering to designate those sugar-beet apostates to our destiny. . . . It is unthinkable that

Originally published in Claude G. Bowers, *Beveridge and the Progressive Era* (Cambridge, Mass.: Houghton Mifflin & Co., 1932), p. 70.

any man should be so little of a statesman and so much of a politician as to throw himself against the current of events in order to take political advantage of what they think is a prejudice of the people in favor of the old Washington dictum about isolation. There is no such thing as isolation in the world today. They say that Cuba is not contiguous; . . . that the Philippines are not contiguous. They are contiguous. Our navy will make them contiguous.

The commercial extension of the Republic has been my dream since boyhood. Eight years ago I read a paper in the Gentlemen's Club in this city on our diplomatic relations in which I outlined the imperial policy we are now beginning and which your letter so eloquently advocates. . . .

Letter of Albert J. Beveridge to Henry D. Estabrook, May 20, 1898. Indianapolis.

. . . Territorial extension is not desirable for itself alone. It is and will be merely an incident of commercial extension. And commercial extension is the absolutely necessary result of the overwhelming productive energy and capacity of the American people. So there you are, and what are you going to do about it?

Originally published in Bowers, *Beveridge and the Progressive Era*, p. 71.

14. "The good Samaritan ... got back his two pence many times over"

GEORGE F. HOAR

Letter of Senator George F. Hoar to the Secretary of the Boston Merchants' Association, December 27, 1898

MY DEAR MR. MOORE:

I fear it will be impossible that I should attend the meeting of the Boston Merchants' Association next Tuesday. . . . If I were to speak on the great subject I should have to express myself with a zeal and earnestness which would very likely carry me beyond the proprieties of such an occasion. Every hour's reflection (and I have given many hours of the most anxious reflection to the subject), impresses me with the great danger of the action proposed by the pending treaty, and with the belief that our safety is to arrest it here. If we would safely escape the greatest peril that ever menaced the Republic we must arrest it here. Do the people of Massachusetts think what the eager and zealous gentlemen who are advocating this new policy of imperialism are asking them to do? . . .

We used to think that our strength came in large part from our unsullied and unequaled public credit; that if, in time of war or public danger we were compelled to contract debt, that the only policy of dealing with it in time of peace was to pay it. But now we are asked to embark on a permanent system of national expenditure which will put this nation under an obligation the equivalent of which will be a national debt greater than that of any other nation on the face of the earth.

Have you ever reflected that a permanent increase of our expenditure of $150,000,000 a year, which we cannot avoid

Hand-corrected carbon copy in G. F. Hoar Papers, Massachusetts Historical Society. Reprinted with the permission of the Society.

and from which we cannot withdraw, is precisely the same thing as adding to our national debt $5,000,000,000 at three percent, which is more than the Government is now paying? I think it can be easily demonstrated that the policies on which we are asked to embark involve a permanent national expenditure much larger than the sum I have named. . . .

This [Imperialism] is proposed to the patriot under the specious guise that the flag is to be honored and made more glorious by a departure from every principle that the flag stands for. It is proposed to the Christian as a new method of civilizing the heathen, as if the heathen were not more likely to be benefited by the good example of the United States in adhering to Christian principles than by having her turn heathen herself to do them good. It is proposed to the merchant and the manufacturer on the specious plea that their trade is to be extended. If the manufacturers and merchants of Massachusetts who have ever read her history or have ever read the history of the country when she has had a share in it are beguiled by this specious sophistry, let them read anew the parable of the good Samaritan, and add another verse:

And lo! the good Samaritan, the child of light, was wiser in his generation than the priest and the Levite, the children of this world, and enjoyed the trade of the man who fell among thieves forever thereafter, and got back his two pence many times over from the profits thereof.

I am, with high regard for the Boston Merchants' Association, faithfully yours and theirs,

GEO. F. HOAR

Imperialism and
the Needs of Military Defense

Theodore Roosevelt versus Edward Atkinson

Considerations of national defense and security determined the position of only a few of the contestants in the Great Debate. For many of them, however, such considerations provided supplementary argument and welcome support. This was true particularly of two of the most dedicated and exuberant of the contestants, Theodore Roosevelt (1858-1919) and Edward Atkinson (1827-1905).

Roosevelt was inspired to defend overseas expansion in the 1890's primarily because of his convictions respecting the international responsibilities of America in an inescapable future, but he was prepared to associate expansion with the military necessities of the present as well as the long-range mission of the Anglo-Saxon race. Edward Atkinson loathed imperialism because it was an enemy of limited government, economical government, and the peaceful expansion of American markets through the natural operation of the law of comparative advantage, but he was equally prepared to associate imperialism with the dissipation of the continental security and military strength of the Republic.

The Roosevelt letters that have been selected are from the years 1897 and 1899, years that bracket Roosevelt's swift and determined rise to national attention. In May 1897 he was a relatively minor official of the McKinley Administration, the newly appointed Assistant Secretary of the Navy. By September 1899 he was an authentic war hero and governor of the most populous state of the Union. His eye was already on the presidency. The evolution of fame and ambition had little affected Roosevelt's convictions respecting the necessities and direction of diplomatic activism. Later the burdens of power would inspire restraint and compromise, but throughout the 1890's Roosevelt was prepared to venture boldly and, more than many of his fellow imperialists, was quick to emphasize the connection between insular expansionism and military strength.

Edward Atkinson had reached his eighth decade by the late 1890's, but age only increased his pugnacity in behalf of the virtue of his own opinions and his determination to seek their wide publication. An industrialist, inventor, and amateur economist, Atkinson was a Bostonian who saw himself as a latter-day Horace Greeley—charged to serve as the nation's school-teacher. A diligent statistician and prolific writer, Atkinson had sought earlier to forward the cause of adult education with pamphlets and speeches in behalf of free trade, sound money, international arbitration, and the science of nutrition. He found his ultimate cause in Anti-Imperialism, and in that cause one of his favorite arguments concerned the "self-evident fact" that expansion would be accompanied by a reduction of the security and strength of the American Republic.

15. "No strong European power ... should be allowed to gain a foothold"

THEODORE ROOSEVELT

Letter of Theodore Roosevelt to Captain Alfred Thayer Mahan, May 3, 1897. Washington, D.C.

Personal and Private

MY DEAR CAPTAIN MAHAN:

This letter must, of course, be considered as entirely confidential, because in my position I am merely carrying out the policy of the Secretary and the President. I suppose I need not tell you that as regards Hawaii I take your views absolutely, as indeed I do on foreign policy generally. If I had my way we would annex those islands tomorrow. If that is impossible I would establish a protectorate over them. I believe we should build the Nicaraguan canal at once, and in the meantime that we should build a dozen new battleships, half of them on the Pacific Coast; and these battleships should have large coal capacity and a consequent increased radius of action. I am fully alive to the danger from Japan, and I know that it is idle to rely on any sentimental good will towards us. I think President Cleveland's action was a colossal crime, and we should be guilty of aiding him after the fact if we do not reverse what he did. I earnestly hope we can make the President look at things our way. . . . I would send the *Oregon,* and, if necessary, also the *Monterey* (either with a deck load of coal or accompanied by a coaling ship) to Hawaii, and would hoist our flag over the island, leaving all details for after action. . . .

Original in Roosevelt Mss., Harvard University. Reprinted by permission of the publishers from Elting E. Morison (ed.), *The Letters of Theodore Roosevelt,* Vols. I & II. Cambridge, Mass.: Harvard University Press, Copyright 1951, by the President and Fellows of Harvard College. Vol. I, pp. 607–8.

... there are big problems in the West Indies also. Until we definitely turn Spain out of those islands (and if I had my way that would be done tomorrow), we will always be menaced by trouble there. We should acquire the Danish Islands, and by turning Spain out should serve notice that no strong European power, and especially not Germany, should be allowed to gain a foothold by supplanting some weak European power. I do not fear England; Canada, is a hostage for her good behavior; but I do fear some of the other powers. I am extremely sorry to say that there is some slight appearance here of the desire to stop building up the Navy until our finances are better. Tom Reed, to my astonishment and indignation, takes this view, and even my chief, who is one of the most high-minded, honorable and upright gentlemen I have ever had the good fortune to serve under, is a little inclined toward it. . . .

Letter of Theodore Roosevelt to George Ferdinand Becker, September 6, 1899. Oyster Bay.

My dear Becker:
... I agree with every word you say as to the excellent effect upon the national character of expansion. A small nation will break down under heavy responsibilities, because it is a small nation; but if a nation is great, as we claim that ours is, it can remain so only by doing a great work and achieving dangerous and difficult tasks. Normally the individual rises to greatness only through labor and strife. As we all know this is invariably the case with the species. In the great majority of cases it is also true of the nation. If we lead soft and easy lives, concerning ourselves with little things only, we shall occupy but an ignoble place in the great world drama of the centuries that are opening. It is only through strife — righteous

Reprinted from Morison (ed.), *The Letters of Theodore Roosevelt,* Vol. I, pp. 1067–68.

strife — righteously conducted, but still strife, that we can expect to win to the higher levels where the victors in the struggle are crowned. . . .

16. "We may not compute the cost of our military control over the Philippine Islands at anything less than 75,000 dollars a day"

EDWARD ATKINSON

From Piety, Politics and Profits: A Public Letter, by Edward Atkinson, December 8, 1898. Boston.

. . . In order to increase our export trade and to complete the work of the war entered upon in the name of humanity but which is degenerating into a war of conquest . . . it is now proposed to pay to Spain twenty million dollars for her claim upon a group of islands of about two thousands in number comprising 150,000 square miles, occupied by eight to ten million people, — mostly savages, a large portion of whom Spain has never been able to subdue in the four hundred or five hundred years of occupancy.

The next step "in the cause of humanity" is to hold these islands under military control in a climate in which white men cannot retain any semblance of health or perform any military duty even for a single year; neither can white men remain there even for a single year without a sacrifice of life in enormous proportion, but in respect to those who survive, the greater part will be disabled every year by fevers of various kinds, by malaria, by small-pox and by another disease due to immorality, of the most malignant kind passing under the same name but specialized by the term "Chinese." Even

Original in Edward Atkinson Papers, Massachusetts Historical Society. Reprinted by permission of the Society.

under the more healthy climate of India and Hong-Kong, the statistics of the British Army disclose the fact that more than five hundred in each thousand men are subjected to this gravest type of venereal disease and that it is necessary to send home every season 4% of the entire force who have been disabled by this disease and must thereafter be supported at the public expense or maintained in hospitals.

The number of American troops which will be required for land service in this military occupation is variously estimated at from 20,000 to 40,000 men. Our standing army in domestic service has heretofore cost over $1000. per man when stationed in healthy climates. According to the estimate of the Secretary-of-War, the appropriations now called for in support of 100,000 men in domestic and foreign service, will come to $1600. per man to which sum must be added the cost of bringing home the survivors of each year's service and sending out the drafted men who will be needed to replace them. I use the word drafted because we may surely assume that there are not a sufficient number of men in this country who are either so ignorant or so hopeless as to induce themselves to commit social or practical suicide as volunteers in this military occupation of tropical islands. This human sacrifice to death or disability by small-pox or by the other nameless disease which I have called "Chinese," by malaria and by fever has not yet sufficed to deter even clergymen who are nominally Christians, from advocating the seizure and permanent retention by military force of these tropical islands. . . .

. . . We may not compute the cost of our military control over the Philippine Islands at anything less than 75,000 dollars a day or something less than 30 million dollars a year which must be raised by taxes in addition to the present taxes together with a large additional sum to make up deficiencies. Our exports to the Philippine Islands, for the past ten years, amount in round figures to $100,000. of domestic goods a year. That sum would suffice to pay the cost to the tax-payers of this country for less than two days military occupation of these islands. I leave to the advocates of what can only be called the venal and venereal policy of occupying these islands under military rule a day beyond the necessity of the case under the responsibilities which we have taken, to compute how much our export trade must be increased from last year's amount, to cover even the cost of occupation. . . .

The Role of Race:
Relationship of Racial Attitudes and the Debate over Expansion

*Alfred Mahan and Henry Adams versus
William James and Charles Francis Adams, Jr.*

The following letters by Alfred Mahan, Henry Adams, William James, and Charles Francis Adams, Jr. will perhaps indicate the complexity of the relationship of racist sentiments and the debate over colonialism in late 19th Century America. There were varying shades of racism evident among the supporters of both sides of that debate, but it would appear that, on balance, sentiments of racial superiority were more prevalent and more pronounced among the Imperialists. Indicative of this fact are the letters of Mahan and Henry Adams, the one an admitted champion of imperialism and concepts of racial superiority; the other a more subtle and self-conscious believer. Adams' brother, Charles Francis, was less smitten by the virus of race consciousness; his anti-imperialist correspondent, Professor William James, was infected not at all.

Mahan has already been introduced; Adams is one of

those men for whom any introduction will prove one-sided and unsatisfactory. It might be sufficient to identify Henry Brooks Adams (1838–1918) as an unhappy, complex, and greatly talented man who was the great-grandson of the second President of the United States. A historian, biographer, novelist, and speculative essayist of large abilities, Adams was also a gossip, an admitted "stable-companion to statesmen," and a man fascinated as well as repelled by the exercise of political power. He was not so much an Imperialist as a friend and fluctuating admirer of many of the leading Imperialists of Washington. He was not a racist by self-admission, but rather the unwilling recipient of the oversimplified classifications of his time and circle.

Adams's brother, Charles Francis (1835–1915), was, in comparative terms, a more simple personality. A civic leader and railroad expert—and a historian of far less originality than Henry—Charles Francis Adams, Jr. was on most issues a moderate. He was temperate in his advocacy of tariff and civil service reform; he was cautious in his advocacy of state regulation of the rates and operations of the railroads. In the cause of anti-imperialism, however, he was prepared to crusade. In that crusade he saw logic in the belief of men such as George F. Hoar and William James that the Malay and Tagalog possessed racial virtues as well as human rights. No Adams was ever a cultural relativist, but Charles Francis came closest to acknowledging the equality of citizens of Quincy and Manila.

William James (1842–1910) was perhaps the only major figure in the debate over imperialism who may be accused of cultural relativism. James, the famous Harvard philosopher and psychologist, was scornful of categorical absolutes in general and the meretricious categories of Social Darwinism in particular. Unconvinced of the inherent virtues of the white race, he had little difficulty believing that the culture of the Polynesian, if distinct from that of the Anglo-Saxon, was not inferior. Each people must possess the right of self-development in the light of its own cultural heritage and aptitudes.

17. "People in the childhood stage of race development"

ALFRED T. MAHAN

Letter from Captain Alfred T. Mahan to Senator Henry Cabot Lodge, February 7, 1899

MY DEAR MR. LODGE:

I shall allow myself the pleasure of congratulating you upon the ratification of the treaty. We have a long row to hoe yet, but I believe that having no two-thirds yoke left on our neck, the country is now fairly embarked on a career which will be beneficent to the world and honorable to ourselves in the community of nations.

I try to respect, but cannot, the men who utter the shibboleth of self-government, and cloud therewith their own intelligence, by applying it to a people in the childhood stage of race development. . . .

Original in H. C. Lodge Papers, Massachusetts Historical Society. Reprinted by permission of the Society.

18. "Foolish Malays"

LETTERS OF HENRY ADAMS

Letters of Henry Adams to Elizabeth Cameron, January 22; January 29; February 5, 1899.

WASHINGTON, January 22, 1899

. . . I turn green in bed at midnight if I think of the horror of a year's warfare in the Philippines . . . where nine men out of every ten in our force must go into hospital, and we must slaughter a million or two of foolish Malays in order to give them the comforts of flannel petticoats and electric railways. . . . We all dread and abominate the war, but cannot escape it. We must protect Manila and the foreign interests, which, in trying to protect the natives from Spain, we were obliged to assume responsibility for. . . . The opponents of the Treaty are unintelligible. They have nothing to propose, and they are inciting the insurgents to insist on our total departure, and even an immediate attack on our troops. . . .

WASHINGTON, January 29, 1899

. . . John Hay coming in to hear my last report from the Philippines—for I am getting up to my neck in Agoncillo's affairs, and every hairy traitor and murderer in the islands of ocean seems to gravitate towards me. Cubans and Philippinos are now running in harness together, and I'm trying to get them all off our hands, and let them murder each other instead of us. . . .

WASHINGTON, February 5, 1899

. . . [They declare] go we must, bag and baggage, and above

Reprinted by permission of the publishers from Worthington C. Ford (ed.), *Letters of Henry Adams* (Boston: Houghton Mifflin & Co., 1938), Vol. II, pp. 208; 211; 215.

all we must hand over Manila! I have had constant communication with them through Rubens, my Cuban manager; and Agoncillo and Luna have frankly said that they were afraid to treat; they would be declared at home to be bribed like Aguinaldo. I am heavy-hearted, not about the Philippinos, who are the usual worthless Malay type, but about the War Department. . . .

19. "The power of self-government ... is assumed to exist"

CHARLES FRANCIS ADAMS, JR.

Letter from Charles Francis Adams, Jr., to Senator G. F. Hoar, January 3, 1899. Boston.

MY DEAR MR. HOAR,

I was much gratified by your's of the 31st. My Lexington paper and Evening *Post* letter will appear in pamphlet form tomorrow, and I shall at once send you copies. . . .

Among other letters, I have received one from Prof. William James, of Harvard, which contains the following paragraph, which may have in it something suggestive for you —

It is your historic way of putting it which gives it such strength as a rallying point. . . . the most bothersome to me is the cant about elevating and liberating these islanders, and advancing them to self-government. We can destroy their old ideals, but we can't give them ours. And the only possible effect of any real influence from us upon them would be their corruption and vice.

. . . the main thing is the direction from which it is approached. You can approach it from the Old World, or despotic side, or you can approach it from the New World, or freedom-of-action side. In the one case, the power of

Original in Papers of G. F. Hoar, Massachusetts Historical Society. Reprinted by permission of the Society.

self-government, or standing alone, is assumed to exist, until the contrary is demonstrated; and even then the dependency is given the least possible direction from without. In other words, everything is assumed in favor of freedom. In the other case, the assumption is against self-government, and the existence of the capacity is admitted, only as it is proved to exist. This is the natural, despotic, and "tutelage" method. As we all know by observation and experience, systems of dependence and "tutelage" invariably tend to become of second nature. In like way, as we equally know, freedom, self-support and independence may be made a second nature. The true American system should be to study to develop this last; and, to develop it, its existence must primarily be assumed. This is the American policy I should recommend. . . .

20. "Could our violent ... irruption into their affairs ... possibly have been as good for them as their own evolution?"

WILLIAM JAMES

Letter from William James to Senator G. F. Hoar, May 11, 1900. Nauheim, Germany.

DEAR SENATOR HOAR,

. . . this is surely our second slavery question; and the country shall have no peace till the infamy is undone.

I confess that I wonder that you can still speak in as friendly a way as you do of the President. Hasn't his policy in this matter (in addition to certainly losing us all our influence in those Islands in the end) lost us our unique past position among nations, of the only great one that could be a trusted

Original in Papers of G. F. Hoar, Massachusetts Historical Society. Reprinted by permission of the Society.

mediator and arbiter, because the only one that was not a professional pirate? Now, (having puked up our ancient national soul after 5 minutes reflection, and turned pirate like the rest) we are in the chain of international hatreds, and every atom of our moral prestige lost forever. Is not this McKinley's responsibility? — Has he not deliberately used the strength of the U.S. to crush what is on the whole the sacredest thing on earth: the successful attempt of an aspiring people to embody its own ideals in its own institutions? Is *anything* of value, that has no roots in history? Could our violent and artificial irruption into their affairs with our remote ideals & habits (even had they submitted without war) possibly have been as good for them as their own evolution? It seems to me that we are playing exactly the part of Attila or Genghis Khan, destroying the life we find, unable to impart new life — and playing this part as a mere improvised & capricious adventure! It is simply hideous! — Finally our President has deliberately and officially adopted the principles of a bunco-steerer and confidence-man in his dealings with Aguinaldo, and unctuously proposed that the nation should recognize them as its avowed policy. . . .

A Poem and a Parody:
Two Englishmen Offer Their Advice

Rudyard Kipling versus Henry Labouchère

21. The White Man's Burden

RUDYARD KIPLING

THE WHITE MAN'S BURDEN

Take up the White Man's burden —
　　　Send forth the best ye breed —
Go, bind your sons to exile
　　　To serve your captives' need;
To wait, in heavy harness,
　　　On fluttered folk and wild —
Your new-caught sullen peoples,
　　　Half devil and half child.

Take up the White Man's burden —
　　　In patience to abide,
To veil the threat of terror
　　　And check the show of pride;

First published in the United States in *McClure's Magazine*, Vol. XII (February, 1899), p. 291.

By open speech and simple,
        An hundred times made plain,
To seek another's profit
        And work another's gain.

Take up the White Man's burden —
        The savage wars of peace —
Fill full the mouth of Famine,
        And bid the sickness cease;
And when your goal is nearest
        (The end for others sought)
Watch sloth and heathen folly
        Bring all your hopes to nought.

Take up the White Man's burden —
        No iron rule of kings,
But toil of serf and sweeper —
        The tale of common things.
The ports ye shall not enter,
        The roads ye shall not tread,
Go, make them with your living
        And mark them with your dead.

Take up the White Man's burden,
        And reap his old reward —
The blame of those ye better
        The hate of those ye guard —
The cry of those ye humor
        (Ah, slowly!) toward the light: —
"Why brought ye us from bondage,
        Our loved Egyptian night?"

Take up the White Man's burden —
        Ye dare not stoop to less —
Nor call too loud on Freedom
        To cloke your weariness.

By all ye will or whisper,
  By all ye leave or do,
The silent sullen peoples
  Shall weigh your God and you.

Take up the White Man's burden!
  Have done with childish days —
The lightly-proffered laurel,
  The easy ungrudged praise:
Come now, to search your manhood
  Through all the thankless years,
Cold, edged with dear-bought wisdom,
  The judgment of your peers.

22. The Brown Man's Burden

HENRY LABOUCHÈRE

THE BROWN MAN'S BURDEN

Pile on the brown man's burden
  To gratify your greed;
Go clear away the "niggers"
  Who progress would impede;
Be very stern, for truly
  'Tis useless to be mild
With new-caught, sullen peoples,
  Half devil and half child.

Pile on the brown man's burden;
  And if ye rouse his hate,

Originally published in *Truth* (London), reprinted in *City and State,* June 1899 (Philadelphia).

Meet his old-fashioned reasons
    With Maxims up to date.
With shells and dumdum bullets
    A hundred times made plain
The brown man's loss must ever
    Imply the white man's gain.

Pile on the brown man's burden,
    Compel him to be free;
Let all your manifestoes
    Reek with philanthropy.
And if with heathen folly
    He dares your will dispute,
Then in the name of freedom
    Don't hesitate to shoot.

Pile on the brown man's burden,
    And if his cry be sore,
That surely need not irk you —
    Ye've driven slaves before.
Seize on his ports and pastures,
    The fields his people tread;
Go make from them your living,
    And mark them with his dead.

Pile on the brown man's burden,
    Nor do not deem it hard
If you should earn the rancor
    Of these ye yearn to guard,
The screaming of your eagle
    Will drown the victim's sob —
Go on through fire and slaughter,
    There's dollars in the job.

Pile on the brown man's burden,
    And through the world proclaim

That ye are freedom's agent —
     There's no more paying game!
And should your own past history
     Straight in your teeth be thrown,
Retort that Independence
     Is good for whites alone.

Pile on the brown man's burden,
     With equity have done;
Weak, antiquated scruples
     Their squeamish course have run,
And though 'tis freedom's banner
     You're waving in the van,
Reserve for home consumption
     The sacred "rights of man"!

And if by chance ye falter,
     Or lag along the course,
If, as the blood flows freely,
     Ye feel some slight remorse,
Hie ye to Rudyard Kipling,
     Imperialism's prop,
And bid him, for your comfort,
     Turn on his jingo stop.

A Final Word from
Two Champion Opponents

Theodore Roosevelt versus William G. Sumner

23. Expansion and Peace

THEODORE ROOSEVELT

It was the gentlest of our poets who wrote:

"Be bolde! Be bolde! and everywhere, Be bolde";
Be not too bold! Yet better the excess
Than the defect; better the more than less. . . .

Captain Mahan, than whom there is not in the country a man whom we can more appropriately designate by the fine and high phrase, "a Christian gentleman," and who is incapable of advocating wrong-doing of any kind, national or individual, gives utterance to the feeling of the great majority of manly and thoughtful men when he denounces the great danger of indiscriminate advocacy of peace at any price, because "it may lead men to tamper with iniquity, to compromise with unrighteousness, soothing their conscience with the belief that war is so entirely wrong that beside it no other

Originally published in the *Independent*, Vol. LI (December 21, 1899), pp. 3401–5.

tolerated evil is wrong. Witness Armenia and witness Crete. War has been avoided; but what of the national consciences that beheld such iniquity and withheld the hand?"

Peace is a great good; and doubly harmful, therefore, is the attitude of those who advocate it in terms that would make it synonymous with selfish and cowardly shrinking from warring against the existence of evil. The wisest and most far-seeing champions of peace will ever remember that, in the first place, to be good it must be righteous, for unrighteous and cowardly peace may be worse than any war; and, in the second place, that it can often be obtained only at the cost of war. . . .

There are men in our country who seemingly forget that at the outbreak of the Civil War the great cry raised by the opponents of the war was the cry for peace. One of the most amusing and most biting satires written by the friends of union and liberty during the Civil War was called the "New Gospel of Peace," in derision of this attitude. The men in our own country who, in the name of peace, have been encouraging Aguinaldo and his people to shoot down our soldiers in the Philippines might profit not a little if they would look back to the days of the bloody draft riots, which were deliberately incited in the name of peace and free speech, when the mob killed men and women in the streets and burned orphan children in the asylums as a protest against the war. Four years of bloody struggle with an armed foe, who was helped at every turn by the self-styled advocates of peace, were needed in order to restore the Union; but the result has been that the peace of this continent has been effectually assured. Had the short-sighted advocates of peace for the moment had their way, and secession become an actual fact, nothing could have prevented a repetition in North America of the devastating anarchic warfare that obtained for three quarters of a century in South America after the yoke of Spain was thrown off. . . .

. . . . .

Wars between civilized communities are very dreadful, and as nations grow more and more civilized we have every reason, not merely to hope, but to believe that they will grow rarer and rarer. Even with civilized peoples, as was shown by our own experience in 1861, it may be necessary at last to draw the sword rather than to submit to wrong-doing. But a very marked feature in the world-history of the present century has been the growing infrequency of wars between great civilized nations. The Peace Conference at The Hague is but one of the signs of this growth. I am among those who believe that much was accomplished at that conference, and I am proud of the leading position taken in the conference by our delegates. Incidentally I may mention that the testimony is unanimous that they were able to take this leading position chiefly because we had just emerged victorious from our most righteous war with Spain. Scant attention is paid to the weakling or the coward who babbles of peace. . . .

The growth of peacefulness between nations, however, has been confined strictly to those that are civilized. It can only come when both parties to a possible quarrel feel the same spirit. With a barbarous nation peace is the exceptional condition. On the border between civilization and barbarism war is generally normal because it must be under the conditions of barbarism. Whether the barbarian be the Red Indian on the frontier of the United States, the Afghan on the border of British India, or the Turkoman who confronts the Siberian Cossack, the result is the same. In the long run civilized man finds he can keep the peace only by subduing his barbarian neighbor; for the barbarian will yield only to force, save in instances so exceptional that they may be disregarded. Back of the force must come fair dealing, if the peace is to be permanent. But without force fair dealing usually amounts to nothing. In our history we have had more trouble from the Indian tribes whom we pampered and petted than from those we wronged; and this has been true in Siberia, Hindustan, and Africa.

Every expansion of civilization makes for peace. In other words, every expansion of a great civilized power means a victory for law, order, and righteousness. This has been the case in every instance of expansion during the present century, whether the expanding power were France or England, Russia or America. In every instance the expansion has been of benefit, not so much to the power nominally benefited, as to the whole world. In every instance the result proved that the expanding power was doing a duty to civilization far greater and more important than could have been done by any stationary power. Take the case of France and Algiers. During the early decades of the present century piracy of the most dreadful description was rife on the Mediterranean, and thousands of civilized men were yearly dragged into slavery by the Moorish pirates. A degrading peace was purchased by the civilized powers by the payment of tribute. . . . But peace did not follow, because the country was not occupied. Our last payment was made in 1830, and the reason it was the last was because in that year the French conquest of Algiers began. Foolish sentimentalists, like those who wrote little poems in favor of the Mahdists against the English, and who now write little essays in favor of Aguinaldo against the Americans, celebrated the Algerian freebooters as heroes who were striving for liberty against the invading French. But the French continued to do their work; France expanded over Algiers, and the result was that piracy on the Mediterranean came to an end, and Algiers has thriven as never before in its history. On an even larger scale the same thing is true of England and the Sudan. The expansion of England throughout the Nile valley has been an incalculable gain for civilization. Any one who reads the writings of the Austrian priests and laymen who were the prisoners in the Sudan under the Mahdi will realize that when England crushed him and conquered the Sudan she conferred a priceless boon upon humanity and made the civilized world her debtor. Again, the same thing is true of the Russian advance in Asia. . . . The Russian conquest of the khanates of central Asia meant the cessation of the barbarous warfare under which Asian civilization had steadily withered away since the days of Jenghiz Khan, and the substitution in its place of the reign of peace and order. All civilization has been the gainer by the Russian advance, as it was the gainer by the advance of France in North Africa; as it has been the gainer by the advance of England in both Asia and Africa, both Canada and Australia. Above all, there has been the greatest possible gain in peace. The rule of law and of order has succeeded to the rule of barbarous and bloody violence. Until the great civilized nations stepped in there was no chance for anything but such bloody violence.

So it has been in the history of our own country. Of course our whole national history has been one of expansion. Under Washington and Adams we expanded westward to the Mississippi; under Jefferson we expanded across the continent to the mouth of the Columbia; under Monroe we expanded into Florida; and then into Texas and California; and finally, largely through the instrumentality of Seward, into Alaska; while under every administration the process of expansion in the great plains and the Rockies has continued with growing rapidity. While we had a frontier the chief feature of frontier life was the endless war between the settlers and the red men. Sometimes the immediate occasion for the war was to be found in the conduct of the whites and sometimes in that of the reds, but the ultimate cause was simply that we were in contact with a country held by savages or half-savages. Where we abut on Canada there is no danger of war, nor is there any danger where we abut on the well-settled regions of Mexico. But elsewhere war had to continue until we expanded over the country. Then it was succeeded at once by a peace which has remained unbroken to the present day. In North America, as elsewhere throughout the entire world, the expansion of a civilized nation has invariably meant the growth of the area in which peace is normal throughout the world.

The same will be true of the Philippines. If the men who have counseled national degradation, national dishonor, by urging us to leave the Philippines and put the Aguinaldan oligarchy in control of those islands, could have their way, we should merely turn them over to rapine and bloodshed until some stronger, manlier power stepped in to do the task we had shown ourselves fearful of performing. But, as it is, this country will keep the islands and will establish therein a stable and orderly government, so that one more fair spot of the world's surface shall have been snatched from the forces of darkness. Fundamentally the cause of expansion is the cause of peace. . . .

Nations that expand and nations that do not expand may both ultimately go down, but the one leaves heirs and a glorious memory, and the other leaves neither. The Roman expanded, and he has left a memory which has profoundly influenced the history of mankind, and he has further left as the heirs of his body, and, above all, of his tongue and culture, the so-called Latin peoples of Europe and America. Similarly to-day it is the great expanding peoples which bequeath to future ages the great memories and material results of their achievements, and the nations which shall have sprung from their loins, England standing as the archetype and best exemplar of all such mighty nations. But the peoples that do not expand leave, and can leave, nothing behind them.

It is only the warlike power of a civilized people that can give peace to the world. The Arab wrecked the civilization of the Mediterranean coasts, the Turk wrecked the civilization of southeastern Europe, and the Tartar desolated from China to Russia and to Persia, setting back the progress of the world for centuries, solely because the civilized nations opposed to them had lost the great fighting qualities, and, in becoming overpeaceful, had lost the power of keeping peace with a strong hand. Their passing away marked the beginning of a period of chaotic barbarian warfare. . . . The fact that nowadays the reverse takes place, and that the barbarians recede or are conquered, with the attendant fact that peace follows their retrogression or conquest, is due solely to the power of the mighty civilized races which have not lost the fighting instinct, and which by their expansion are gradually bringing peace into the red wastes where the barbarian peoples of the world hold sway.

24. The Conquest of the United States by Spain

WILLIAM GRAHAM SUMNER

Lecture before The Phi Beta Kappa Society of Yale University, delivered January 16, 1899.

During the last year the public has been familiarized with descriptions of Spain and of Spanish methods of doing things until the name of Spain has become a symbol for a certain well-defined set of notions and policies. On the other hand, the name of the United States has always been, for all of us, a symbol for a state of things, a set of ideas and traditions, a group of views about social and political affairs. Spain was the first, for a long time the greatest, of the modern imperialistic states. The United States, by its historical origin, its traditions and its principles, is the chief representative of the revolt and reaction against that kind of a state. I intend to show that, by the line of action now proposed to us, which we call expansion and imperialism, we are throwing away some of the most important elements of the American symbol, and are adopting some of the most important elements of the

First published in pamphlet form by Dana Estes and Co., Boston, 1899.

Spanish symbol. We have beaten Spain in a military conflict, but we are submitting to be conquered by her on the field of ideas and policies. Expansionism and imperialism are nothing but the old philosophies of national prosperity which have brought Spain to where she now is. Those philosophies appeal to national vanity and national cupidity. They are seductive, especially upon the first view and the most superficial judgment, and therefore it cannot be denied that they are very strong for popular effect. They are delusions, and they will lead us to ruin unless we are hard-headed enough to resist them. . . .

There are some now who think that it is the perfection of statesmanship to say that expansion is a fact, and that it is useless to discuss it. We are told that we must not cross any bridges until we come to them; that is, that we must discuss nothing in advance, and that we must not discuss anything which is past because it is irretrievable. No doubt this would be a very acceptable doctrine to the powers that be, for it would mean that they were relieved from responsibility, but it would be a marvellous doctrine to be accepted by a self-governing people. . . . Within a year it has become almost a doctrine with us that patriotism requires that we should hold our tongues whenever our rulers choose to engage in war, although our interests, our institutions, our most sacred traditions, and our best established maxims may be trampled underfoot. There is no doubt that moral courage is the virtue which is more needed than any other in the modern democratic state, and that truckling to popularity is the worst political vice. The press, the platform, and the pulpit have all fallen under this vice, and there is evidence that the university also, which ought to be the last citadel of truth, is succumbing to it likewise. I have no doubt that the conservative classes of this country will yet look back with great regret to their acquiescence in the events of 1898 and the doctrines and precedents which have been silently established. Let us be well assured that self-government is not a matter of flags and Fourth of July orations, nor yet of strife to get offices. Eternal vigilance is the price of that as of every other political good. The perpetuity of self-government depends on the sound political sense of the people, and sound political sense is a matter of habit and practice. We can give it up and we can take instead pomp and glory. That is what Spain did. She had as much self-government as any country in Europe at the beginning of the sixteenth century. The union of the smaller states into one big one gave an impulse to her national feeling and national development. The discovery of America put into her hands the control of immense territories. National pride and ambition were stimulated. Then came the struggle with France for world-dominion, which resulted in absolute monarchy and bankruptcy for Spain. She lost self-government, and saw her resources spent on interests which were foreign to her, but she could talk about an empire on which the sun never set, and boast of her colonies, her gold mines, her fleets and armies and debts. She had glory and pride, mixed, of course, with defeat and disaster, such as must be experienced by any nation on that course of policy, and she grew weaker in her industry and commerce, and poorer in the status of the population all the time. She has never been able to recover real self-government yet. If we Americans believe in self-government, why do we let it slip away from us? Why do we barter it away for military glory as Spain did?

There is not a civilized nation which does not talk about its civilizing mission just as grandly as we do. The English, who really have more to boast of in this respect than anybody else, talk least about it, but the Phariseeism with which they correct and instruct other people has made them hated all over the globe. The French believe themselves the guardians of the highest and purest culture, and that the eyes of all mankind are fixed on Paris, from whence they expect oracles of thought and taste. . . . The Spaniards have, for centuries, considered themselves the most zealous and self-sacrificing

Christians, especially charged by the Almighty, on this account, to spread true religion and civilization over the globe.
They think themselves free and noble, leaders in refinement
and the sentiments of personal honor, and they despise us as
sordid money-grabbers and heretics. . . . Now each nation
laughs at all the others when it observes these manifestations
of national vanity. You may rely upon it that they are all
ridiculous by virtue of these pretensions, including ourselves.
The point is that each of them repudiates the standards of the
others, and the outlying nations, which are to be civilized,
hate all the standards of civilized men. We assume that what
we like and practice, and what we think better, must come as
a welcome blessing to Spanish-Americans and Filipinos. This
is grossly and obviously untrue. They hate our ways. They
are hostile to our ideas. Our religion, language, institutions,
and manners offend them. They like their own ways, and if
we appear amongst them as rulers, there will be social discord
on all the great departments of social interest. The most
important thing which we shall inherit from the Spaniards will
be the task of suppressing rebellions. If the United States
takes out of the hands of Spain her mission, on the ground
that Spain is not executing it well, and if this nation, in its
turn, attempts to be school-mistress to others, it will shrivel
up into the same vanity and self-conceit of which Spain now
presents an example. . . . Now the great reason why all these
enterprises, which begin by saying to somebody else: We
know what is good for you, better than you know yourself,
and we are going to make you do it — are false and wrong, is
that they violate liberty; or, to turn the same statement into
other words: the reason why liberty, of which we Americans
talk so much, is a good thing, is, that it means leaving people
to live out their own lives in their own way, while we do the
same. If we believe in liberty, as an American principle, why
do we not stand by it? Why are we going to throw it away to
enter upon a Spanish policy of dominion and regulation?

The United States cannot be a colonizing nation for a long time yet. We have only twenty-three persons to the square mile in the United States without Alaska. The country can multiply its population by thirteen, that is, the population could rise above a billion, before the whole country would be as densely populated as Rhode Island is now. There is, therefore, no pressure of population, which is the first condition of rational expansion, and no other reason for it. . . . In the second place, the islands which we have taken from Spain never can be the residence of American families, removing and settling to make their homes there. The climatic conditions forbid it. . . .

Spain stands, in modern history, as the first state to develop and apply a colonial system to her outlying possessions. Her policy was to exclude absolutely all non-Spaniards from her subject territories, and to exploit them for the benefit of Spain, without much regard for the aborigines or the colonists. . . . A modern economist stands aghast at the economic measures adopted by Spain, as well in regard to her domestic policy as to her colonies. . . . We now hear it argued that she is well rid of her colonies, and that, if she will devote her energies to her internal development, and rid her politics of the corruption of colonial officials and interests, she may be regenerated. That is a rational opinion. It is the best diagnosis of her condition, and the best prescription of a remedy which the occasion has called forth. But what, then, will happen to the state which has taken over her colonies? I can see no answer except that that nation, with them, has taken over the disease, and that *it* now is to be corrupted by exploiting dependent communities just as she has been. That it stands exposed to this danger is undeniable. . . .

The Americans have been committed from the outset to the doctrine that all men are equal. We have elevated it into an absolute doctrine as a part of the theory of our social and

political fabric. It has always been a domestic dogma in spite
of its absolute form, and as a domestic dogma it has always
stood in glaring contradiction to the facts about Indians and
Negroes, and to our legislation about Chinamen. In its absolute form it must, of course, apply to Kanakas, Malays, Tag-
als, and Chinese just as much as to Yankees, Germans, and
Irish. It is an astonishing event that we have lived to see
American arms carry this domestic dogma out where it must
be tested in its application to uncivilized and half civilized
peoples. At the first touch of the test we throw the doctrine
away, and adopt the Spanish doctrine. We are told by all the
imperialists that these people are not fit for liberty and
self-government; that it is rebellion for them to resist our
beneficence; that we must send fleets and armies to kill them,
if they do it; that we must devise a government for them, and
administer it ourselves; that we may buy them or sell them as
we please, and dispose of their "trade" for our own advantage. What is that but the policy of Spain to her dependencies? What can we expect as a consequence of it? Nothing but that it will bring us where Spain is now.

But, then, if it is not right for us to hold these islands as
dependencies, you may ask me whether I think that we ought
to take them into our Union, at least some of them, and to let
them help to govern us. Certainly not. If *that* question is
raised, then the question whether they are, in our judgment,
fit for self-government or not is in order. The American
people, since the civil war, have to a great extent lost sight of
the fact that this state of ours, the United States of America,
is a confederated state of a very peculiar and artificial form. It
is not a state like the states of Europe, with the exception of
Switzerland. The field for dogmatism in our day is not theo-
logy; it is political philosophy. "Sovereignty" is the most
abstract and metaphysical term in political philosophy. No-
body can define it. For this reason it exactly suits the purposes of the curbstone statesman. He puts into it whatever he
wants to get out of it again, and he has set to work lately to
spin out a proof that the United States is a great imperialistic

state, although the Constitution, which tells us just what it is, and what it is not, is there to prove the contrary. . . .

What was at first only a loose combination or alliance has been welded together into a great state by the history of a century. Nothing, however, has altered that which was the first condition of the Union, viz., that all the States members of it should be on the same plane of civilization and political development; that they should all hold the same ideas, traditions, and political creed; that their social standards and ideals should be such as to maintain cordial sympathy between them. The civil war arose out of the fact that this condition was imperfectly fulfilled. At other times actual differences in standpoint and principle, or in ideals and opinion, have produced discord within the confederation. Such crises are inevitable in any confederated state. It is the highest statesmanship in such a system to avoid them, or smooth them over, and, above all, never to take in voluntarily any heterogeneous elements. The prosperity of such a state depends on closer and closer sympathy between the parts in order that differences which arise may be easily harmonized. What we need is more intension, not more extension.

It follows, then, that it is unwisdom to take into a state like this any foreign element which is not congenial to it. Any such element will act as a solvent upon it. Consequently, we are brought by our new conquests face to face with this dilemma: we must either hold them as inferior possessions, to be ruled and exploited by us after the fashion of the old colonial system, or we must take them in on an equality with ourselves, where they will help to govern us and to corrupt a political system which they do not understand, and in which they cannot participate. From that dilemma there is no escape except to give them independence and to let them work out their own salvation. . . .

. . . . .

Another phenomenon which deserves earnest attention from the student of contemporaneous history and of the trend

of political institutions, is the failure of the masses of our
people to perceive *the inevitable effect of imperialism on
democracy.* . . .

Everywhere you go on the Continent of Europe at this
hour you see the conflict between militarism and indus-
trialism. You see the expansion of industrial power pushed
forward by the energy, hope, and thrift of men, and you
see the development arrested, diverted, crippled, and defeated by measures which are dictated by military considerations. At the same time the press is loaded down with
discussions about political economy, political philosophy, and
social policy. They are discussing poverty, labor, socialism,
charity, reform, and social ideals, and are boasting of enlightenment and progress, at the same time that the things which
are done are dictated not by these considerations, but by
military interests. It is militarism which is eating up all the
products of science and art, defeating the energy of the population, and wasting its savings. It is militarism which forbids
the people to give their attention to the problems of their own
welfare, and to give their strength to the education and comfort of their children. It is militarism which is combating the
grand efforts of science and art to ameliorate the struggle for
existence.

The American people believe that they have a free country, and we are treated to grandiloquent speeches about our
flag and our reputation for freedom and enlightenment. The
common opinion is that we have these things because we
have chosen and adopted them, because they are in the Declaration of Independence and the Constitution. We suppose,
therefore, that we are sure to keep them, and that the follies
of other people are things which we can hear about with
complacency. People say that this country is like no other,
that its prosperity proves its exceptionality, and so on. These
are popular errors which in time will meet with harsh correc-
tion. The United States is in a protected situation. It is easy
to have equality where land is abundant, and where the popu-

lation is small. It is easy to have prosperity where a few men have a great continent to exploit. It is easy to have liberty when you have no dangerous neighbors, and when the struggle for existence is easy. There are no severe penalties, under such circumstances, for political mistakes. Democracy is not then a thing to be nursed and defended, as it is in an old country like France. It is rooted and founded in the economic circumstances of the country. The orators and constitution-makers do not make democracy. They are made by it. This protected position, however, is sure to pass away. As the country fills up with population, and the task of getting a living out of the ground becomes more difficult, the struggle for existence will become harder, and the competition of life more severe. Then liberty and democracy will cost something if they are to be maintained.

Now what will hasten the day when our present advantages will wear out, and when we shall come down to the conditions of the older and densely populated nations? The answer is: war, debt, taxation, diplomacy, a grand governmental system, pomp, glory, a big army and navy, lavish expenditures, political jobbery, — in a word, imperialism. In the old days the democratic masses of this country, who knew little about our modern doctrines of social philosophy, had a sound instinct on these matters, and it is no small ground of political disquietude to see it decline. They resisted every appeal to their vanity in the way of pomp and glory which they knew must be paid for. They dreaded a public debt and a standing army. They were narrow-minded and went too far with these notions, but they were at least right, if they wanted to strengthen democracy.

The great foe of democracy now and in the near future is plutocracy. Every year that passes brings out this antagonism more distinctly. It is to be the social war of the twentieth century. In that war militarism, expansion, and imperialism will all favor plutocracy. In the first place, war and expansion will favor jobbery, both in the dependencies and at home. In the second place, they will take away the attention of the people from what the plutocrats are doing. In the third place, they will cause large expenditures of the people's money, the return for which will not go into the treasury, but into the hands of a few schemers. In the fourth place, they will call for a large public debt and taxes, and these things especially tend to make men unequal, because any social burdens bear more heavily on the weak than on the strong, and so make the weak weaker and the strong stronger. Therefore expansion and imperialism are a grand onslaught on democracy. . . .

The laws of nature and of human nature are just as valid for Americans as for anybody else, and if we commit acts, we shall have to take consequences, just like other people. Therefore, prudence demands that we look ahead to see what we are about to do, and that we gauge the means at our disposal, if we do not want to bring calamity on ourselves and our children. We see that the peculiarities of our system of government set limitations on us. We cannot do things which a great centralized monarchy could do. The very blessings and special advantages which we enjoy, as compared with others, bring disabilities with them. That is the great fundamental cause of what I have tried to show throughout this lecture, that we cannot govern dependencies consistently with our political system, and that, if we try it, the state which our fathers founded will suffer a reaction which will transform it into another empire just after the fashion of all the old ones. That is what imperialism means. . . .

My patriotism is of the kind which is outraged by the notion that the United States never was a great nation until in a petty three months' campaign it knocked to pieces a poor, decrepit, bankrupt old state like Spain. To hold such an opinion as that is to abandon all American standards, to put shame and scorn on all that our ancestors tried to build up here, and to go over to the standards of which Spain is a representative.

Bibliographical Note

The following list is in no sense a formal bibliography. It is rather a list of some two dozen articles that the editor of this volume would have liked to have reprinted had space permitted. One of the purposes of this series of readings is to encourage further exploration in the primary sources. For the topic of Imperialism and Anti-Imperialism in the 1890's, such exploration might well start with the following essays:

Charles Francis Adams, Jr., "Imperialism and 'The Tracks of Our Forefathers' " (pamphlet published by Dana Estes and Co., Boston, 1899).

George S. Boutwell, "The President's Policy: War and Conquest Abroad, Degradation of Labor at Home" (pamphlet published by the American Anti-Imperialist League, Chicago, 1900).

J. G. Carlisle, J. R. Procter, G. L. Rives, and Donelson Caffery, "The Policy of Expansion — Cuba and the Philippines," *Harper's Weekly Magazine,* Vol. XLII (October 22, 1898), pp. 1027–46.

Andrew Carnegie, "Americanism Versus Imperialism," *North American Review,* Vol. CLXVIII (March 1899), pp. 362–72.

Andrew Carnegie, "Distant Possessions — The Parting of the Ways," *North American Review,* Vol. CLXVII (August 1898), pp. 239–48.

Eugene Tyler Chamberlain, "The Invasion of Hawaii," *North American Review,* Vol. CLVII (December 1893), pp. 731–35.

Charles Denby, "Shall We Keep the Philippines?", *Forum,* Vol. XXVI (November 1898), pp. 279–81.

E. L. Godkin, "Samoan Troubles," *The Nation,* Vol. LVIII (May 17, 1894), pp. 358–59.

J. P. Gordy, "The Ethics of the Panama Case," *Forum,* Vol. XXXVI (July 1904), pp. 115–24.

George F. Hoar, "Our Duty to the Philippines," *The Independent,* Vol. LI (November 9, 1899), pp. 2995–3000.

Willis Fletcher Johnson, "Justice and Equity in Panama," *Forum,* Vol. XXXVI (July, 1904), pp. 125–37.

A. Lawrence Lowell, "The Colonial Expansion of the United States," *The Atlantic Monthly,* Vol. LXXXIII (February 1899), pp. 145–54.

John T. Morgan, "The Territorial Expansion of the United States," *The Independent,* Vol. L, Part II (July 7, 1898), pp. 10–12.

Henry C. Potter, "National Bigness or Greatness—Which?" *North American Review,* Vol. CLXVIII (April 1899), pp. 433–44.

John R. Procter, "Hawaii and the Changing Front of the World," *Forum,* Vol. XXIV (September 1897), pp. 34–45.

Whitelaw Reid, "The Territory with Which We Are Threatened," *The Century Illustrated Monthly Magazine,* Vol. LVI (September 1898), pp. 788–94.

George A. Richardson, "The Subjugation of Inferior Races," *Overland Monthly,* Vol. XXXV (January 1900), pp. 49–60.

James Schouler, "A Review of the Hawaiian Controversy," *Forum,* Vol. XVI (February 1894), pp. 670–89.

Carl Schurz, "Thoughts on American Imperialism," *The Century Illustrated Monthly Magazine,* Vol. LVI (September 1898), pp. 781–88.

William M. Springer, "Our Present Duty," *North American Review,* Vol. CLVII (December 1893), pp. 746–52.

John L. Stevens, "A Plea for Annexation," *North American Review,* Vol. CLVII (December 1893), pp. 736–45.

Benjamin R. Tillman, "Bryan or McKinley: Causes of Southern Opposition to Imperialism," *North American Review,* Vol. CLXXI (October 1900), pp. 439–46.

Hermann E. Von Holst, "Some Lessons We Ought to Learn," *University of Chicago Record,* Vol. III, No. 46 (February 10, 1899), pp. 299–304.

Stephen M. White, "The Proposed Annexation of Hawaii," *Forum,* Vol. XXIII (August 1897), pp. 723–36.

BOOK MANUFACTURE

Imperialists Versus Anti-Imperialists: The Debate Over Expansionism in the 1890's was composed by Allied Typesetting Company, Dexter, Michigan. Printing and binding was by NAPCO Graphic Arts, Inc., Milwaukee, Wisconsin. The internal design was by the F. E. Peacock Publishers, Inc. art department. Evelyn Hansen designed the cover. The type is Times Roman.